'THE PRACTICAL ISLANDER': R. M. Lockley in his own words

Some of the many books by R. M. Lockley:

Dream Island (1930)
Island Days (1934)
I Know an Island (1938)
Early Morning Island (1939)
The Way to an Island (1941)
Inland Farm (1943)
The Island Farmers (1946)
Letters from Skokholm (1947)
The Cinnamon Bird (1948)
The Golden Years (1950)
Pembrokeshire (1957)
The Naturalist in Wales (1970)
Myself When Young (1979)
Dear Islandman (with Ann Mark) (1996)

‘The practical islander’: R. M. Lockley in his own words

Jen Llywelyn (editor)

First published in 2010

Jen Llywelyn (editor)

Published with the financial support
of the Welsh Books Council

ISBN: 978-1-84527-303-3

Cover design: Sion Ilar

Published by Gwasg Carreg Gwalch,
12 Iard yr Orsaf, Llanrwst, Wales LL26 0EH
tel: 01492 624031
fax: 01492 641502
email: books@carreg-gwalch.com
website: www.carreg-gwalch.com

Editor's dedication:

To my parents,
for introducing me to Pembrokeshire,
and to the world of nature
that R. M. Lockley also loved.

Contents

Foreword

When I was asked to write a foreword to this collection from some of my father's publications I thought how difficult it would be to comment objectively on his writing, so many sentiments are involved in close relationships. Father always said his children and grandchildren were his severest critics, but we all agree that his written observations and his knowledge of natural history were where his talents lay. The excerpts Jen Llywelyn has selected here show her obvious love of those same subjects, which makes my job much easier.

I suppose I had rather a unique childhood, although at the time I did not realise it. I certainly enjoyed life on Skokholm (except the numerous occasions when my fearless parents chose to go to sea in very stormy weather). In order to keep the wolf from the door Father started writing books and articles about his life on Skokholm and its birds, and as a result the island became well-known as Britain's first Bird Observatory.

In his earliest books Father largely glosses over our financial woes and other hardships. He describes an idyllic life, which it was in many ways. The reason for such embroidery was perhaps because he had this dream of one day producing a best-selling novel.

When we started farming after we had to leave Skokholm in 1940 because of the war, subsequent books on our island experiences are painted less glamorously. The co-operative farming experiment was a failure; Father admitted he was the wrong person to run such a venture, and knowing him as I do, I have to agree. He had this innocent and naïve inability to see that his plans, however appropriate, might not meet with everyone's approval, just as our criticism of something he had written was greeted with a look of hurt.

My father kept a diary from 1921 until 1992. These, I hope one day to put into book form. They are full of his observations and his daily activities, his restlessness and his wish to be forever pioneering. Even on the days when he was beset with frustrations of one kind or another, I find, faithfully recorded, some comment on the land, the birds and the flowers he loved so much.

Ann Mark
New Zealand, April 2010

Introduction

One of the first books I fell in love with was *Early Morning Island* by R. M. Lockley. It is the story of island life through the eyes of a little girl, Ann, with photographs of her playing with her ponies, Soay sheep and goats, and talking with the seabirds who also lived on the island of Skokholm, which lies off Pembrokeshire in south Wales. Ann is R. M. Lockley's daughter.

I must have read this book thousands of times, and through it I acquired a feel for island life. I so badly wanted to be Ann! I discovered that R. M. Lockley had written other books. My grandfather, a countryman, and my uncle, a farm manager, had also read several, and loved them.

It was not until the 1990s that I acquired *Inland Farm* (1943) and learned so much about farming in Wales during the Second World War – the difficulties, the bureaucracy, the changes, and the farming community Ronald Lockley set up near Newport in Pembrokeshire. I was thrilled by the clarity of his writing, by his willingness to be experimental in order to help the 'war effort', and by his descriptions of the wildlife of the area.

I have since bought more of R. M. Lockley's books, and I love them so much that I want to share Ronald's writing with others. This book seeks to tell his story in his own words, from six of his books (he wrote, or was in some way involved in, over fifty). It was not easy – there is considerable overlap, but also many seeming puzzles, and finding a cohesive chronology was challenging. It is hoped that the notes linking the extracts will close gaps and provide some illumination – some gleaned from other books and some from Ann – where Ronald leaves us in the dark.

There is also the fact of his enhancement of history . . . For example, in one early book, Ronald paints his mother as a 'penniless widow', bringing up a family alone. Later we discover that his father was in fact alive, but was for most of the time absent from the family home because he was an inveterate gambler! Presumably in the earlier book Ronald wished to avoid publicising his father's faults.

But despite – or perhaps because of – Ronald's eccentricities he is worth reading. His writing takes us on voyages with him, onto islands peopled and not, hearing and seeing the natural world, and particularly birds and wild flowers. He uses various local names for some of these; he is inconsistent with spellings. I have left them as he wrote them. His writing is natural and sparkling. It is right and proper that he should be introduced to a new audience.

As a countrywoman myself, I find it sad that Ronald had seen 'scores' of yellowhammers and linnets in Wales comparatively recently. He would be hard-pressed to find many now. Certainly the corncrake is gone from the fields around Cardiff: the method of harvesting from the outside of a field to the inside, as condemned by Ronald in his boyhood, has been responsible for us losing many birds and small animals. Nowadays the RSPB is encouraging farmers to change their practice and start in the middle of a field, giving the animals a chance to run for cover. There are still corncrakes to be seen (and definitely heard) in the north of Scotland and on Coll and Tiree, for example, but very few elsewhere in Britain.

Ronald Lockley was born in St Mellon's, Cardiff, in 1903, the youngest of six children. His father's gambling habit meant that Mrs Lockley had to run a private school to make ends meet. On leaving Cardiff High School Ronald set up a small poultry farm and began 'building' islands. In 1927 he discovered the island of Skokholm, off Pembrokeshire, and decided he would live there. He leased the island and set up home for himself and a couple of helpers. Notwithstanding the scepticism of the local people, Ronald loved island life, just as he had thought he would, and quickly learned about boats, seabirds, and carpentry.

In 1928 he married Doris, an old friend from St Mellon's; later, Ann was born, and was brought up on the island. An idyllic life for the three of them – but then came war, and they were instructed to leave Skokholm. Sadly they took their animals and left, and found Inland Farm, near Newport in Pembrokeshire, and later Island Farm – whose name, confusingly, is far too similar to that of Inland Farm; even more confusingly it is not on an island but on the sloping promontory of Dinas Head (sometimes known as Dinas Island), between Newport and Fishguard. The reader needs to bear this in mind!

Ronald became a renowned naturalist and ornithologist. His intention was partly to supplement his income and support his family, but he was a natural communicator, and his writing can transport the reader to Skokholm, or Bardsey, Heligoland, or even to London's stuffy streets. The extracts chosen tell of his life from birth until just after the war, and concentrate on his three main loves: the natural world, farming, and most of all, islands.

In 2006 the island of Skokholm, which had been a bird observatory since the mid 1930s, was bought by the Wildlife Trust for South and West Wales. The Trust is refurbishing the living accommodation. Soon it will again be possible to take a three or four-night break there, experiencing island life in a pretty basic form. But not nearly as basic as Ronald found it when he first landed there in 1927, and as is described later in this book.

In 2009, to my joy I managed to find Ann, the star of *Early*

Morning Island, living in New Zealand. She has been a great support in writing this book, and has contributed the Foreword. My very special thanks to her for her friendship now – and for introducing me, so many years ago, to the special treasure that is island life.

Jen Llywelyn
Trisant, Ceredigion
March 2010

1

The first islands
(1903–1920)

The Way to an Island, *which was published in 1941, tells of Ronald Lockley's early life near Cardiff, and the beginning of his fascination with islands. The story begins with a few pages about his siblings:Enid, Kenneth, Kathleen, Aline, and, younger than Ronald, Marjorie. There were ten years between them.*

Following an accident with a frightened pony, Ronald (aged about five) was confined to bed for over a month. During this time, his great friend, Margaret – the pony was owned by her family – brought him a copy of Swiss Family Robinson *to read. He was already interested in islands, and called the book* 'an ideal appetiser for islands when you are very young'. *He also tried* Robinson Crusoe, *but found it more difficult to read at that stage of his life:*

Robinson Crusoe is full of the disappointments which islanders, and indeed most of us, experience far more often than we enjoy successes. And because of this truth I found myself in later life turning to read the grim struggle of Robinson Crusoe more often, until at last the smug self-satisfied *Swiss Family Robinson* lay unopened on my bookshelf. When I first began on Crusoe's adventures I found myself apt to skip the early and later parts containing his adventures with the outside world. I lost interest in him when he began to stray from his island, and I resented very much the introduction of savages and bloodshed. That sort of stuff belonged, I thought, to the wild west novels – any one can make up a yarn about blood and cannibals and sudden death. I preferred the hero to continue with his interesting farm, his goats, the birds he saw, his crops, and the quiet adventures and walks alone on the island.

I got through both books while I was in bed, and went on to read Ballantyne's *Coral Island*; and here again it was the story of the boys' adventures in living on and exploring the island that succeeded best with me – I scarcely read the pirate and murder chapters. The three books cured me better than the doctor's prescription for my weak thigh. And when Margaret came to see me I talked of the island I was going to live on when I grew up.

Margaret, who was a little younger than Ronald, and who planned to become a lady doctor, asked Ronald how he would get a living on an island.

I told her I hoped to be a naturalist. A naturalist, I said, finds out new kinds of birds and flowers and animals. He travels widely, from the North Pole and Greenland to the tropics. I told her that if she married me I would find her useful – since she wanted to handle limbs and bones – to skin birds and animals for my museum. When I had made enough money I would retire to an island, probably in the Hebrides, and there I would set up my museum, one each of every bird, animal, and egg in the world – one only – the rest of the island would be a preserve for every kind of living bird and beast I could secure. It would be fun, I said, to see how many different kinds would be able to live there. British animals would have special preference, to preserve them in case they were exterminated elsewhere. My keepers would have orders to shoot nothing, not even vermin like stoats and weasels and eagles. Margaret listened indifferently – she thought it would be nice to have a pretty yacht in which to sail about the island. She would probably keep a lot of horses and dogs on the island, she thought. I wasn't so sure about that, but I said nothing. I thought I should probably remain single after all.

A few years later, Ronald became interested in birds. This began by accident: when his mother insisted he eat everything on his plate, he devised a system of hiding a paper bag in his trouser pocket and filling it with his unwanted food. He would then throw it through a gap in the playground wall, and watch the birds – who would be waiting for him – quarrelling over their dinner. He borrowed books from the village library and began to be able to tell the difference between song thrush and mistle thrush, and between crow, rook and jackdaw.

By the time I was ten years old I knew every common bird intimately, and could tell any one what bird it was flying overhead or slipping through the branches of the fruit trees. But people seldom troubled to ask me – it was considered a queer and rather stupid pastime. 'Stupid old birds, what can you see in them?' I would be asked.

So I kept my discoveries to myself . . . When birds were lacking in the garden I turned to wild flowers, to the weeds which every one else tore up if they saw them with seeing eyes. I collected into my own garden the best looking of them: corn marigold, scarlet pimpernel, bindweed, mallow, and white campion. By degrees I could name them, though often with difficulty, and with many trials and errors. I had no one to share their mystery with, but that made a secret which I delighted to hug to myself. I was a strange boy, people said, going after birds, and looking at flowers instead of playing cricket, staring like an idiot into the heart of a flower for minutes on end, straining to look at the tiny yellow and brown migratory warblers feeding in the trees, with a troubled look because I could not identify these so-alike atoms.

In August 1914, Mrs Lockley rented a cottage by the sea, in Amroth in Pembrokeshire, for a long family holiday. Previously they had not been able to afford holidays – their father's gambling debts made sure of that – but Mrs Lockley's private school was doing well.

Ronald described the holiday cottage thus:

It was an old building, placed on the side of a hill amid flowers, fruit, vegetables, and chickens. It was the poet's cot, with its beehive's hum, and below us, a willowy brook in a field of rushes and rabbits. Every morning before the others were awake I would creep out to watch the rabbits feeding and playing in the dew. I would appear at breakfast breathless with news of what I had seen – but the others scarcely troubled to listen. They had more important news to discuss: what excursion would be taken that day, the local gossip, and the terrible news of war in Europe.

Our holiday had to be shortened. There was a scare of food shortage – bread could not be got in the village. Grave news came from France and Belgium. The local yeomanry mobilized and swept past on horseback, splendid in khaki and white cord, scattering the yellow-hammers which droned from the high banks of the lanes. And brother Ken, who was now sixteen, boldly declared he was seventeen and joined the army forthwith. We felt that the Germans were in for a bad time.

On returning home to Cardiff, Mrs Lockley got Mr Witcombe, a neighbouring farmer, to plough her allotment, and started growing vegetables for the family. She took the children blackberrying:

. . . to make hundreds of pounds of jam to help feed the family and the school boarders. We marched with our baskets to the Wenallt, a mountain slope over-looking Cardiff. Thousands of nut bushes clothed the slopes too. Some of us were not too particular about the blackberries; as long as we filled the bottom of the basket, and made a showing that way, we felt entitled to eat to our hearts' content, and for the rest it seemed more important to explore, to play Indians, and to blaze trails through the bush. I ran after rabbits, watched weasels and squirrels, and more than once stood with a tingling feeling in my hair watching an adder basking on some warm stone or tree-stump.

Ronald started at Cardiff High School. After being ill in bed again for three months, this time after appendicitis, Ronald set off to explore the outdoors again – the family was now holidaying at Southerndown, on the coast near Bridgend. He met a hedgehog one day, and was able to get close to it, and was fascinated by all the bright red fleas hiding between the hedgehog's prickles.

I wondered if the animal found some means of destroying the parasites – certainly it could not scratch the skin under that spiny back.

It was a small adventure, but exciting to one so long banished from the wild. And soon, as I crept through the aisles of ash and oak, came the second small adventure – the quiet voice, the sub-song of the willow-warbler. The loud sweet cadence of spring had gone, and the bird seemed practising it over in a whisper. Sometimes it broke off in the middle, as if dissatisfied with the technique, and went back to the beginning, to play this over and over again, adding, as it seemed to me, a new note here and there, and only once completing the song I knew so well, and which it would not sing again with a full throat until next April. But I watched the bird trying these autumn notes as it sat preening on a twig over my head, and there was deep joy in me as I looked at an old friend.

Next morning I was out again before the sun rose, and I turned inland to a moor with nothing but sheep and stonechats and singing yellow-hammers for company. I had my breakfast with me (having arrived so late yesterday for the meal that I'd been advised to take it next time or do without it), and so there was no call for hurry. I lingered in the sandy valleys of the moor till the sun came burningly out, and I could eat to the sight of butterflies and the song of the humble-bees. The grasshoppers started an endless tune. Drowsy with food and warmth I threw myself full length in the bracken, and dreamed and slept.

I woke refreshed. The sun was now very high and very hot. I saw a wood on the slope of a hill, and climbed to it gladly, after drinking at a stream in the rushy bottom.

Ring-doves flew out with a blue clatter as I approached, and I once more caught the notes of the willow-warbler's sub-song. Then loud and clear came the 'tiff-too-ee, tiff-too-ee' of the chiff-chaff, close cousin of the willow-warbler. Now a chiff-chaff should not sing in August, according to the bird books which I had read. I was astonished and pleased. Here was a contravention of a law laid down by man. The chiff-chaff sang on persistently, telling me that he was governed by no man-made laws. He sang to me with notes that look commonplace enough on paper, but uttered from that green-yellow form swaying in the wind which threaded the oak and ash and larch the notes came to me rich with all the joyousness of life, and all the beautiful mystery too.

I pushed on into the gloom of the pines, glad of the coolness. Deeper and deeper in, the silence growing, and the flowers giving way to a bed of pine needles. Here was solitude, even loneliness, since the only life that spoke was the hushing voice of the wind in the tree-tops, remote and uneven like the sea on a distant strand.

Suddenly I realised I was staring into the eyes of an extraordinary slice of life – at first I thought it was a cat, then some strange and lovely carving, some golden vase. It was a long-eared owl, which, seated on a pine branch, had drawn itself up to its greatest length and height, so as to appear as unlifelike as possible. The upright mottled-eared one looked at me with narrowed eye-slits, unmoving and unmoved. I had never seen an owl of this kind before, but I was allowed to gaze my fill and satisfy myself that it was according to the picture in the book of birds. Only of course it was beautiful with life.

The sun warmed my cold legs and arms as I reached the moor again. A small hawk came swinging low past me in the valley. It was joined by another, and the pair began to play together. Their play became a mock fight, one pursuing the other with dazzling turns and speed, diving, twisting, and mounting as with the same impulse. One was bluer than the other. They were both scarcely larger than blackbirds. These things told me I was seeing my first merlins.

For a long time I lay in the sandy grass watching the merlins at their games over the burning valley. Then they were gone, arrows from Diana's bow.

I walked home. At the table I exploded my bombshell among the family:

'I saw a long-eared owl and two merlins this morning.'

The bombshell did not explode. Enid said: 'It's extraordinary what nerve Alice has got.' (She was referring to the servant-girl.) 'She's out every night with a soldier!'

'I saw her sit herself down between two soldiers yesterday on the cliffs, as cool as you like,' said Aline.

And the gossip rolled on, crushing my owl and merlins out of existence, as far as the family was concerned.

Ronald's life continued in quite lonely fashion. He found few people to share his love for nature. A school-friend, Ted, wanted to collect birds' eggs, and Ronald, on the promise of half the spoils, took Ted out to where he knew there were nests. Ted wanted eggs simply as acquisitions, but Ronald's conscience got the better of him when he saw the beauty of a great tit's nest and he began to value the eggs more in their natural place. He sold his collection of eggs, and used the money to buy books.

I had to confine myself to second-hand and shop-soiled books, ranging in price from a shilling to three and sixpence. They were all natural history books. The smaller booksellers and second-hand dealers came to know and tolerate me as I skirmished through their shelves. I perused some of the expensive books little by little each day until I had read them right through without buying them. On birthdays and at Christmas I would have enough money to buy a seven-and-sixpenny book. I remember buying one such book which I had already read through twice in the shop; I thought then that any book that could not stand a third reading was not worthy of being called a book.

At night, then, I was not lonely. I could lie in bed and stretch out my hand in the dark to feel the friends on my shelf. I could pick out each one by its shape and place, and then, lighting the gas jet, I could read to my heart's content. I could open each unhesitatingly almost exactly at the paragraph I wished to consult, so often had I read and re-read each volume. I could quote copiously from these books, but I did so only to myself, for I should have been ridiculed if I had attempted to quote to anyone I knew.

The only time I was ever warned off handling books in a shop was when two pet mice escaped from my sleeve and ran behind the shelves, and were not recaptured until the stall had been dismantled. The women attendants shrieked, I turned as red as a turkey-cock's wattle, and the manager wrote a letter of protest to my mother. As he gave it to me to hand over, I felt justified, as a good customer of his, in burning it when I lit a cigarette in the train on the way home.

Three days after my fifteenth birthday the armistice of the Great War was signed. The news came to expectant boys at lessons in [Cardiff] high school. There was a short assembly, and we were allowed to rush out into the streets to join the gone-mad crowds. With others I boarded an empty lorry going into the city. We danced and capered and shouted. We rushed into Woolworth's and bought threepenny whistles and 'submarine' hummers. And forming ranks with strangers, men and women, we marched through the streets, singing Welsh songs, whistling them, and then breaking off to dance, to jump on overloaded cars, to throw our caps at policemen who laughed back at us. We built a tower of caps on one policeman's helmet, and cared not when they toppled over and were trodden underfoot.

The soldiers evacuated the school, and the mistresses, who had never been able to control the more unruly boys, gradually made way for returning masters. The headmaster now warned us in assembly that the moral tone of the school was going to be tightened, if necessary by the use of the cane. Any one reported to him was 'for it'. And the next day my beloved mice, which had only just got me into trouble at the bookshop, let me in 'for it'.

I happened to be playing with one of my mice under the lid of my desk, in order to relieve the tedium of angles and tangents. Our desks were movable – on tiny inset wheels, that shrieked for lack of oil if set in motion. As I bent down to rescue a mouse that had strayed down my trouser leg, I accidentally shoved the desk. A horrible squeak betrayed me.

Miss Rose said acidly: 'Stand up at once, Lockley.'

I stood up, while the mouse ran over my knee and gave me the most excruciating sensations as it clawed my bare skin. I couldn't bear it another moment, and, bending down, I grabbed the mouse and thrust it, under cover of the desk, into my trouser pocket. Miss Rose turned scarlet as I again accidentally shoved the desk in my haste. It squeaked fiercely.

'How dare you!' she said, and sitting down she wrote a note swiftly. 'Lockley, take this to the headmaster at once.'

Poor Ronald received 'six of the best' from the headmaster, simply for pushing a desk!

In 1919, the family went to spend the summer at Southerndown again (just before the signing of the Versailles Treaty). Ronald and Marjorie, his youngest sister, went wandering in the fields and woods, and along the sea shore, enjoying exploring the limestone terraces on the beaches there. They saw butterflies and dragonflies, and stalked corncrakes in the clover fields. They found rock-pipits' nests on the limestone terraces – one with chocolate-coloured eggs in, and one with red eggs.

I am ashamed to say that I broke my promise to my little and loving sister. She had made me say I would not rob the nests of the rock-pipits. But the wish to show them at school, and the hope of selling them well, sent me sneaking after them the day before we left Southerndown. At school I sold the chocolate eggs as rock-pipits' for eightpence each, and the curious red eggs I sold at a shilling each as shore-larks'. My naming was accepted without question – I was considered the expert.

It was the end of egg-collecting for me. A month later, in July, two charming little birds came and built in the Virginia creeper that covers most of Milford House School, our Whitchurch home. The soft slight nest, made of wool, string, and moss, and lined with fine hair, was placed on a ledge of masonry below the window of my bedroom, and was completely concealed by the leaves of the creeper. There the hen laid three eggs while the cock sat on the top of a copper beech at the entrance gates; there he caught flies and winged insects all day, and carried them to his sitting wife. Every time I leaned out of the window to look at the nest he grunted a soft warning to her, and she would fly out and join him. They were a splendid pair, and their trust (as it seemed to me) in us was touching. I decided I would take but one egg.

That one egg lay in my collection for two days, while I spent a sleepless night fighting my conscience. At the evening of the second day I returned it to the nest. I could not bring myself to prick it and blow it. And I have never blown an egg since.

Ronald spent the next couple of weeks watching the spotted flycatchers (whom he named Muscicapa and Grisola, from the Latin name of the species) raising their young – but the egg he had taken from the nest didn't hatch. The boy got a reputation for strangeness after sitting hidden in the garden shrubbery observing the birds – 'Unjust inferences were made accordingly', *he commented.*

On the twelfth day the youngsters flew out of the nest when, leaning out of the window, I parted the leaves to look at them. One fluttered into a small fir tree and was safe, but the other alighted on the ground. Immediately the household cat walked towards it, evil inquiry in every motion of his crouching body.

I looked about desperately for a weapon to hurl at puss. I was upstairs, of course. I yelled at him, but all my efforts were in vain. The flycatchers themselves had taken the matter in hand. The hen flew down to the grass a few inches from puss's nose, and uttered feeble cries of distress. Puss was drawn to bigger game, and crouching lower still, began a stealthy advance upon the fluttering adult. The nestling meanwhile hopped towards the shrubs, out of immediate danger.

I now feared for Grisola's safety. I grabbed a hairbrush from the room, and was about to throw it down on the cat when I saw that he was in full chase after Grisola, while Mr Muscicapa came fluttering behind, pecking visciously at the cat's tail! It was an astonishing sight. A second later Grisola looped up over the cat's head and joined her husband with an arrow-like swoop upon puss's back. They both pecked and stabbed to such effect that the bewildered animal ran hissing from the lawn. And thus these minute birds set to flight their formidable enemy.

I searched for the missing nestlings, and replaced them in their nest, holding my hands over them until they were quiet there. I did not look again, for fear of a repetition of the incident. In early August the flycatchers joined the swifts, which suddenly left the village eaves. They disappeared on their autumn journey to Africa.

The next year, 1920, Ronald should have been studying for his matriculation exams – he had a correspondence course to take at home – but instead he was out and about, and often hiding from the world in the little hut he'd built for himself on a tiny island (he called it Moorhen Island) in a nearby river, not far from the Melingriffith tin works.

Midsummer found me listening in ecstasy to the song of the wood-warbler, which seemed to me to express all the joy of the life of the tree-tops in the time of their fullest burgeoning.

'See-ee-ee-ee-ee-ee-ee!' cried the wood-warbler in his vibrating voice, and his whole body shivered with delight. A million leaves in the tops of the trees swayed in a rustling chorus which swamped the last sighing notes of the singer. Yes, yes, this is the time we dreamed of in the long wait and coolness of winter, the time of contentment and friendliness and fullest perfection. And with my heart full of a rare joy I waited for the three bell-like notes which concluded the wood-warbler's song. They seemed to round off that astonishing magic madrigal by giving utterance to the sadness of replete happiness.

'Pí!'

Ah! The exquisite pain of consummation!

'Pí!'

Ah! This happiness is too much!

'Pí!'

Yes, he who holds the overflowing cup in his two hands has tears in his eyes.

There were often tears in mine when I caught sight of the sunshine-coloured singer moving from branch to branch through the lofty canopy.

Ronald continued to study for his matriculation, but spent a great deal of time in his little hut on Moorhen Island. He described one of his walks there.

That greenfinch's nest was unusual – built entirely of fresh young groundsel, a loose, shallow cup of stalks and heads, no doubt hurriedly built by the hen to accommodate her five pretty spotted and streaked eggs. The bright green cock, flashing yellow panels in the wing, displayed in a curious flapping flight, in which the wings seemed to be used alternately, while he sang his long-drawn happy trill redolent of summer sunlight. I watched him feed his sober-coloured mate near the nest. He fondled and 'kissed' her beak with his heavy bill, as he passed to her a pap of semi-digested seed gathered from the abundant wild flowers and weeks of Witcombe's fields.

Leaving the oat-field I stepped into the lane, shadowed with oaks, leading to the Melingriffith tinworks, and the bridge over the canal. Here a group of tall elms was occupied by an immense rookery; assembled cawing rooks took little notice of men hammering at tin sheets in the sheds fifty yards below. The rooks' nests were all in trees without low branches, a wise provision against egg-collecting boys. About these bare trunks the songs of nesting robin, wren and chiffchaff would be heard in a lull between the gusty chorus of cawing from above.

In the wall which retained the lane above the canal were rows of drainage holes which, opening above the slow-moving water, had been adopted by the sand-martins. All day long dozens of these brown-grey, white-breasted swallows dipped and flirted in the air over the water, calling with a pleasant liquid note, carrying feathers to the holes, and sometimes dusting luxuriously in the dry earth of the tow-path. They wheeled about me at first, calling excitedly, but if I remained still long enough they ignored me and got on with their private affairs. I never ceased to wonder at the close juxtaposition of the hideous smoking tinworks and its row of slum cottages, and the brilliant company of the birds about and above the canal.

The towpath was my narrow way to the perfection of Moorhen Island. I followed it with slow steps, slow because I relished every yard of this delicious walk. Gradually I left behind the uproar of cawing rooks, twittering sand-martins, clucking hens and quacking ducks. Above the cottages, the newly-arrived swifts screamed as they swooped under the loose tiles and rotting roofs where they were soon to nest. The last impression of this crazy corner was reassuring – at the end of the narrow-gauge tramline stood a disused steam-engine with grass growing out of its smoke-box, and hedge-parsley hiding its rusted wheels.

Low marshy fields were on my left as I walked northwards, and on my right, across the canal, were the hanging woods, the woods at whose foot was hidden my island and hut, and where I hoped to hear the long overdue blackcap. It might not be easy to catch his notes, so great already was the orchestra of bird-song between field and water and wood. I could hear the blackbird, the song-thrush, the mistle thrush, the robin, the wren, the chiff-chaff, the willow-warbler, the hedge-sparrow, the whitethroat, the chaffinch, the greenfinch, and bigger, less continuous singers, such as the cuckoo, green woodpecker, and ring-dove.

There was about a mile of this walk along the towpath, with the rough fields on the left and the woods on the right. Then came a lock and the lock-keeper's cottage beside it. A hundred times I had wished to be the lucky occupier of this charming home. He was a tinplate worker, and his wife attended to the few barges which now, at rarer and rarer intervals (as road transport competed more and more successfully with water transport), entered and left the lock. He and his lived on the island made by the canal and the race of the surplus water, an island which enclosed a large garden humming with bees. I saw a great tit picking up the dead bees that the live bees were turning out at the spring-cleaning of the hives. The cottage path was lined with daffodils and violets, and in a small field between my wood and the lock there were ducks and chickens and grazing goats.

I crossed the field and was at last at home in my well-beloved wood. Although April was far spent and May at hand, the tangle was still but thinly leafed, and so I moved cautiously, 'freezing' against a tree if anyone passed along the towpath, now on the other side of the canal. I stayed quite as still when the passer-by was only a bullfinch, a squirrel, a rabbit, a willow-warbler. And the bullfinch, puffing his crimson breast out and pausing to scratch his black skull-cap, considered, if he bothered to think about me at all, that I was but a harmless dead tree-stump. Indeed, I learnt to stand so still that at times birds perched on me, often a robin or a willow-warbler, more rarely a wren, once a yellow-hammer; blackbirds have searched for worms between my feet, and bees and butterflies have visited the flowers in my hands.

I was drawing out my plank bridge when I saw the russet-red brow of a hen blackcap. Hens usually arrive a few days after the cocks, to whom they are drawn by the persistent singing of their future mates. I stood still and waited, hoping to see my lord of the black cap. The hen watched me for a moment, but as I was so quiet she began again her search for insects in the low brambles. She flew to the island, and I saw her moving in jerks over the top of my thatched hut. She vanished the other side, and almost immediately I heard the vigorous and charming song of her mate. I hastily set the plank, and not bothering to draw it over with me, I walked softly towards the singing bird. Yes, there he was, in the branches of a sallow, whiter of breast than his hen, with a strikingly jet cap placed rather forwardly on his brow. He quite outsang the chiff-chaff in the willow. But he could not stay still for long. He dropped down into the tangle where the hen was hidden, and I lost them both in that lovely environment of bluebells and anemones, kingcups and golden saxifrage. His voice soon came again, a hurried burst of sprightly notes from the alders on the 'mainland'.

Nearer, a pair of tree-creepers chased about a rotting willow-trunk. I caught the faint, seldom-heard ripple of song uttered by this mouse of a bird. For once it was giving way to the general exhilaration of the springtime woods; for once it had abandoned its everlasting prying and running after tree-dwelling insect life.

2

Lundy and Skomer

(about 1921)

Ronald Lockley knew that he would fail his matriculation exam because he'd spent most of his time on nature study. He was very worried about his mother's reaction. She had, after all, paid for the correspondence course he was supposed to be taking! He wanted to travel, to go at least to a nearby island, but didn't have pocket money.

Ronald worked a bit for George Witcombe, the neighbouring farmer, a Somerset man who'd migrated to Wales. The boy enjoyed the work, feeding the pigs and hens or cleaning the stables, but concealed this from his mother because she would have considered it below his social station to work as a farm labourer. Occasionally Witcombe paid him a small amount for his work.

One day, he saw that a steamer was going to sail to Lundy Island in the Bristol Channel. The fare was ten shillings and sixpence. He hatched an idea – to get to the island, get a job on the farm there, and write to his mother to tell her he was staying, and that she was well rid of him. He was about seventeen years old at this time.

I managed to raise the fare in a fortnight of scraping. I was short on the last day, so I rode into Cardiff and sold some of my text and lesson books to a second-hand bookseller. Mother packed me an excellent picnic lunch, and I embarked at Cardiff docks at 9.30 a.m. I was wearing a mackintosh, and I also carried the indispensable *Manual of British Birds*. With these things I felt I could face the whole world.

It was 22nd July, and above the ship gulls hovered in the blue like big flakes of snow. A few of the black-headed gulls still wore their chocolate-coloured hoods. A mute swan cygnet floated in the filthy water of the dock, begging for bread with a graceful motion of its head and neck. I was in a fine humour until the wind began to freshen in the channel. Off Minehead the steamer began to roll. At Lynmouth it was plunging so violently that it was impossible to disembark passengers. It was my first experience of sea-sickness. The sea-birds no longer held my interest. I lay on the deck and shut my eyes and wished I had never left home. After a while I even wished I was dead. At Ilfracombe I might have abandoned the steamer and gone a-roving in Devon – if the quietness of the harbour had not brought me to my feet, thinking myself a cured man. But the horrid retching sensations returned as we steamed north for Lundy.

I lay against the rail in misery.

Never did land seem so desirable as the pebble beach under the high cliffs of Lundy. And never had I seen water of so rich and clear a blue – you could see the weeds and stones far down under the lifeboat that brought us ashore, as islanders do in tales of coral islands. I may as well admit that the first sensations on landing were those of a great hunger, not for the island, but for food. It was 3 p.m., and my early breakfast had long been sacrificed to the fishes. However, I was determined to get out to the west side (we had landed on the south-east point) and look at the sea-birds before I started to eat. I therefore raced up the steep cliff path, and crossed fields with singing larks and stone-chats, until I reached the west coast.

Ronald ate his lunch, entranced by the sight of gulls, guillemots and razorbills, oyster-catchers and kittiwakes, and many puffin burrows – but no puffins. Then he heard the steamer's siren announcing that it was time to return.

I had had no time to carry out my plan to see the farmer and ask him if he would take me as a worker. I had had no time to visit the farm, which I supposed was there among a group of buildings, including a church, which I could see in the distance. I had had less than an hour on the island, and now the wretched steamer was recalling me. Somehow, too, I felt I would not care to live on Lundy. It was too sophisticated, with a steamer landing scores of visitors on a fine day in summer; with its church and two lighthouses, and farm and small village, it was too inhabited. No, for me it would be enough if an island had only one house and that my own, just one 'lone shieling on the misty island'. And with these excuses I obeyed the summons of the ship's siren.

As we left Lundy Roads a great flight of long-winged, black-backed, white-breasted birds skimmed northwards. They were the first Manx shearwaters I had ever seen. I wondered whither they were bound. Apparently they were not interested in Lundy. They were more likely headed for the Pembrokeshire islands of Skomer and Skokholm, about forty miles to the north. As I watched those great black and white swallows of the sea skimming so effortlessly over the rough water I wondered if it would be possible to live on one of those little-known Pembrokeshire islands. Some time ago I had copied their outlines from large-scale maps in Cardiff library, and I knew their topography almost by heart: Ramsey with her twin hills; Skomer with her grand cliffs and countless birds (already renowned in bird-books as the chief home of the Manx shearwater); Skokholm, smaller and lower and least reported; Grassholm, the smallest and remotest, and home of the only colony of gannets or solan geese in England and Wales; and Caldey, the island with a monastery and a village, and therefore least attractive of all to me.

A fortnight later Ronald's longing for the islands took him, with two friends, Eric and Edward, to a small hut on the coast of Pembrokeshire, not far from St David's. One morning, early, he was wakened by a high-pitched, plaintive call, and crawled out of the tent to see his first buzzard.

I had no idea this fine hawk still survived in Pembrokeshire. Books had told me it was only found in the wilds of mid-Wales. But here were two, floating over our camp, within gunshot. I shook Eric and Edward, and they came out to stare with me at the broad gold and brown wings of the soaring buzzards. Long I stared, and the others were getting dressed when I was still staring, for a third buzzard had joined the pair, and I could not look long enough on their aerial play. They spiralled up on an up-draught of air, until they were hard to see against the pale blue of the morning sky. Gulls came into the same pocket of rising air, and feeling its power, allowed themselves to be drawn up into the sky on motionless wings until they, too, became mere dots in the blue of heavens.

The buzzards came every morning and evening to the camp, picking up the entrails from rabbits we had snared which we placed on a rock for them. And almost as vividly I remember the scores of yellow-hammers which piped from every furze bush in the treeless valley of Caerbwdy. August is seemingly one of the best months for the singing of the yellow-hammer. They droned from sunrise until after the first stars of evening, and were most insistent early in the morning. I heard their ceaseless 'Bit-o'-bread-and-no-cheeeese' as I lay under the blankets on my heap of bracken; I heard it with joy before my eyes were opened. And I heard the mewing of the buzzards mingle with it and the pratings of scores of linnets.

During that time in Pembrokeshire, Ronald also enjoyed choughs, kestrels, wheatears, and some seals basking on the rocks below the cliff. He fell in love with Pembrokeshire then, and regretted leaving the county.

When he returned home to Cardiff, it was harvest-time. And his penchant for wild-life conservation got him into a dangerous situation.

The machine [a reaping and binding machine] whirred round and round the oats, drawing closer and closer to the centre, in which were gathered the frightened rabbits and corncrakes. This was the hour I dare not miss. Helpers were gathering up heavy sticks to attack the wild things that would at the last moment dash for freedom. And I, trembling for them, but fascinated, must needs be there to watch.

We had not many swathes to cut when, as I walked closely behind the reaper-and-binder, I suddenly saw a young corncrake in the straw in front of the humming knife. Without thinking of myself I sprang over the knife to rescue it. It was the nearest thing to committing suicide – as I was told afterwards. Old George's prompt action saved me. He yelled 'Jump! with such ferocity and suddenness that I automatically jumped. The knives whirred under my feet, and I tumbled over into the uncut oats while he stopped his scared team.

Then old George got down and turned the full stream of his blasphemous wrath on me. He roared it out, and I, realizing at last how narrow my escape had been, cowered down in the oats, thoroughly ashamed of my foolish impulse. We were both, in fact, badly shaken. Witcombe had to call his son to carry on with the driving of the machine, while he adjourned to the hedge and steadied himself with a long draught of his favourite Somerset cider from a huge stone jar.

After going to London to take – and fail – his matriculation exam, Ronald got the train back to Wales. On the way he decided once again to leave home, and become 'an honest, self-respecting wayfarer . . . I would wander over the hills of Wales, earning a day's crust and a rest for my body at some poor needy farmer's, always helping the oppressed . . .' *So rather than going to Cardiff, he got off at Newport and visited a pawnbroker. He got rid of everything but his* Manual of British Birds *and his mackintosh, and bought an ex-army rucksack and other bits and pieces – including a cap, for disguise. He then got a train to Brynmawr and the Brecon Beacons, with the thought of trying to find a job on a farm.*

I got a corner seat and held to it, furtively studying the other travellers who began to fill up the compartment. Six colliers and two women came in – they had evidently been shopping in town and were now going back to their home valleys. There was a smell of beer. The train started.

One collier addressed me in Welsh, but a woman at once interrupted. 'Speak you English, mun,' she said to him. 'Can't you see the gentleman is English?' And without waiting for him to do so, she asked me: 'You shall not mind if we do sing, boy bach?'

I smiled and nodded encouragement, though I was secretly disappointed that I still seemed to look so much a gentleman. Well, when my clothes got a bit more dirty and torn I would pass for the tramp I wished to be. As for singing, all train travellers up and down the Welsh valleys (and Whitchurch had been on the Taff Vale route) were used to the delightful singing of the Welsh miners.

The long dreary journey through the smoky valleys was brightened by the traditional songs of the Welsh people, and my heart was greatly lifted as my feet beat time to the splendid rhythm. I knew the airs, but not the words, and this fact added to the enjoyment and gave the songs a pleasant sense of mystery.

This was probably the high-spot of Ronald's adventure. After an evening at the fair with a young girl in Brynmawr, and a snowy night sleeping rough in a hay-loft, he decided that he was being unfair to his mother, and began walking the fifty or so miles back to Whitchurch.

The thrill of the fox-hunt takes up most of one chapter in The Way to an Island. *It is a wonderful description of the meet, and the progression of the hunt. But although Ronald was used to killing rabbits for food, he was sickened by the digging-out and killing of the fox, and expressed his fury to the Master.*

When it became public that he had failed matriculation, Ronald managed to persuade George Witcombe to rent part of his farm to him. Ronald wanted to keep bees and goats, but since Witcombe couldn't abide either, Ronald kept chickens, and still spent many hours on Moorhen Island.

I was at peace that summer, drawing health and joy from the fields and the woods alternately. My enclosure was bordered on one side by one of Witcombe's straggling hedges, and the length of this (for which I paid rent as part of the rood) became a special joy. The greenfinches, chaffinches, and linnets which nested in the hedge took on a special interest because they were under my hands. And as the wild hedge-plants crept from bud to flower and fruit I grew to know each plant and love it. By July the hedge was a sight with the long trailers of the tufted vetch climbing in company with honeysuckle and black bryony. Below these the deep purple woundworts mingled with hemp nettles and campions, and the multi-coloured blackberry flowers. Corymbs of ragwort made golden intervals along the hedge, and at the foot were the humbler blossoms of field pansies, wheats, mallow, and St John's wort. At night I sometimes went out to watch the silent moths visiting the clusters of the night-flowering campion, whose snow-white petals seemed to shine in the dim light.

The worst part of farming was the selling of produce. People haggled with you, and I was too sensitive to argue – rather than that I'd give the stuff away.

Later, I wrote out rules for living. They were simple: just two:

(1) Be natural.
(2) Be intelligent.

Under Rule (1) I amplified the instruction as follows: 'Wear as few clothes as possible: rather thick and few than thin and many. Leave off your shoes and socks. Your hair your hat. Wash your body daily. Sleep always in the open air; sleep only to rest. Eat moderately the simple food. Be happy; there has never been occasion for moroseness.'

And under Rule (2): 'Appreciate, know, and love the ways of natural life. Speak only words of true meaning. Sneer not, but point out, not the mistakes, but the true way. Be moderate in thought and deed; smile, but do not laugh. Use your life intelligently; do not waste time. Think more and write less. Take sufficient unto the day only; be not over-provident. Harness no creature to the machines of man; it will lose caste.'

If only I had followed these rules with more devotion!

I tried to at first. I slept much out of doors in that fine

summer, generally in the back garden, but I often stole away, after the others were in bed and the house silent, to Moorhen Island, and there, rolled in an old blanket, I dozed away the midsummer darkness, such as it was.

But before the lark had risen at four a.m. summer time I might be walking through the woods in bare feet, living up to my rules at least for those few rich morning hours, with the celestial music in my heart now. And the life of the woods and fields flowed like a river of poetry about me.

But one day a couple of lads from the tin works found his hut, and destroyed it, thinking an old tramp was living in it. They stole his old books, including a copy of Swiss Family Robinson. *Ronald was there when they came back, and was about to attack them in his anger, but they laid about him instead. He tried to burn down what remained, but it was too damp.* 'It was a long time before I revisited those woods.'

For a while Ronald Lockley tried hard to find his niche in the world. He tried growing and selling herbs, without much success. He did fall in love, for a while, however – unrequitedly – with the girl in the herbalist's shop. Then he began practising austerities like eating dry brown bread and drinking only water. But still the island dream persisted: 'There were other schemes, but always I returned to the favourites: North Rona or the herb farm.' *(No community had inhabited North Rona in the Hebrides since 1680, when it is thought an invasion of rats ate the stored food.)*

I happened to pick up a biography of Tolstoy, and having read something of the man I began eagerly to read his works, wading through his interminable novels and wonderful narratives. Tolstoy confirmed the need for austerity. But soon Turgenev widened my view. I became more tolerant as the philosophies of Walt Whitman, Emerson, Ruskin, Ibsen, Shaw, Arnold Bennet, and others penetrated my thick skull. Each in turn impressed my impressionable mind, and I worshipped each as I read, and until the next author came along to dethrone his predecessor. I seemed to sit on a stage with an audience of a hundred authors shouting their wares at me, demanding to be read. Read my philosophy first! Read my theory! Read my economy! Read my criticism! Read my Utopia! Read my poetry! Read my idealism! Read my realism!

The sum total of this demonstration was: 'Read, you ignorant numbskull!' And read I did.

I began my education at last.

Then Ronald had the chance to buy ten acres of land in the Beggan Valley. He jumped at it. His mother came up with the money – £650 – and they built a little house on the land, for Ronald and his sister Enid to live in. He started with poultry as the easiest way to make initial money before branching out, though he didn't care for poultry farming and was aware of how horrible poultry farms can look.

My farm would be different. Once I had paid off the mortgage on the land I would convert the fields into a wild-bird-and-flower-filled paradise on earth. My island should take form – since any other way seemed denied to me at present – in the centre of a large pond, which I was planning in the marshy lower field. The old oak there would crown the island with its noble head. The island will be my wild garden, loved alike by bird and flower. I planned to raise a high bank steeply over the water in one spot, and prod holes in it as a start for the burrowing sand-martins. Perhaps kingfishers would come if I could encourage minnows, and of course there would be several sorts of wagtails. I would have a seont wall over part of the pond, with moss and toad-flax, and hand-holes for birds' nests. For the moorhens and wild ducks there would be islets and clumps of flag and reed and rush, and low bushes would attract the sedge-warblers and whitethroats and blackcaps. About the mainland shores of the pond I would plant a low wood of alder and sallow and willow, to bring back all the birds I knew and loved so well in Moorhen Island woods.

But the planning and the anticipation were almost – and I thought so even then – more pleasant than the realization.

The ten acres of the farm became an island for me, and I recorded every movement of bird and flowering plant from day to day. It was a struggle to keep up with the flowers at midsummer, when my notebooks were filled with observations and lists of things seen. A July day in 1923, for instance, records these in bloom in my hedges: Small Upright St John's Wort, Rest-Harrow, Nipplewort, Self-Heal, Hooded and Common Bindweeds, Poppy, Navew, Common Knapweed, Hedge-Mustard, Musk, Mallow, Wood-Sage, Water-Figwort, Shining Cranesbill, Yellow Rattle, Small-flowered Willow-Herb, and Yarrow. All the flowers were given capital letters in those pages, by the worshipping nature-lover.

* * *

On fine summer nights I took my bed and slept out of doors. I woke one morning to find a yellow-hammer – the one with a nest by the stream – singing from my pillow. And a lark came regularly to hunt for food about the foot of the bed.

There was a beautiful little wood on the side of the hill above me, and there, one year, a nightingale, a scarce bird in the west country, nested. I listened to its song with disappointment – it has been, I think, badly overrated. But that it sang at night it would have been overlooked by the ordinary person who cared little for birds. A blackbird singing at night is ten times more enthralling.

One spring morning, after a night of heavy rain, the stream burst its banks and flooded the hollows of the lower field, filling to the brim my moat, and leaving the oak and the heaped-up earth around it en-isled. It was a pleasant glimpse of what my island and moat would look like when finished. And next morning I was overjoyed to find seven handsome shelducks parading on the steep shore of the island. Now the true haunt of this most handsome of British ducks is the sea – and I felt honoured and gratified by this apparent recognition of my efforts to import the atmosphere of sea and island into the country.

I peeped from behind the hedge and watched what the lovely creatures were up to. White necks, beetle-green heads, and splendid chestnut-red breast bands, they walked in solemn file along the shore, inspecting the rough holes and crevices of the heaped-up earth. A wild hope that they might stay and nest filled my mind, and I vowed to dig some holes as an encouragement for them. But suddenly they seemed to catch sight of me, and they rose up into the air, the ducks quacking and the drakes whistling musically.

Oh, that rich whistle! It spoke to me of the sea and sandbanks where the surf rolled in, white and clean and healing!

As the shelducks sailed overhead and moved off to the sea, ten miles beyond the valley, I longed to go with them. My longing for a real island in the sea came back to me with great strength. The quiet beauty of the Beggan Valley in early May seemed dull and tasteless that day. And the long rolling pipes of the blackbirds only filled me with a deeper wish.

* * *

Thoughts of an island home never left me. In the next summer, with the farm running smoothly, I could arrange to leave the Beggan Valley and commence my search in earnest. A friend came with me and we went down to Pembrokeshire. We arrived late one night in the little sea-valley of Caerbwdy, where I had camped years before.

We might have gone to explore Ramsey Island, lying off this headland of St David's, but we found the local Welsh boatmen wanted a lot too much for the mile crossing – at least we thought their charge for visiting an inhabited island too much. Ramsey had a large farm, and its neat cultivated appearance put me off visiting it. I wanted to get to wilder places. In the south of St Brides Bay Skomer and Skokholm were unfarmed and derelict. In my pocket I had a hand-drawn enlargement of a map of Skokholm, and though I had never set foot there, I knew every creek and contour of this lonely little island.

We moved to Marloes, to find ourselves in a country where a rich dialectic English is spoken. There is no Welsh spoken in the south half of Pembrokeshire, which was settled by Flemish and Norman immigrants after the native Welsh had been driven out by the Norman barons. A line of castles divides the country from west to east, castles built by the invaders to keep the Welshmen in the hilly north of the county. So the south part of Pembrokeshire, a smiling low undulating land of cornfields and sweet pasture, is known today as 'Little England beyond Wales'. Old Flemish-style chimneys, bake-ovens, shovels, and even some words from the Flanders speech will be found in South Pembrokeshire today.

From Marloes, Ronald and his friend managed to get a boat to

Skomer – the sea was too wild to go to Skokholm on that occasion. The family then living on Skomer – the Sturts – gave them permission to wander the island. They saw myriad sea-birds, and the flowers were at their best. When darkness fell, they sat down to eat their picnic.

As we ate our food, we heard strange grunting noises coming from under the earth. The noise gradually increased as the excited shearwaters sensed the approaching night. But it was getting on for midnight before any came out of the burrows to meet the shearwaters which were returning from the sea. We tried to tell each other what the noise sounded like – a hybrid between a strangled cock-crow and a long-drawn-out human wail of distress was the final and not very satisfactory diagnosis. Each bird had, it seemed, its own dialectic cackle. The whole gradually expanded to one continuous roar by half-past midnight, and the swish of wings passing over our heads mocked the fainter notes of the wind in the outcrops of rock.

We wandered over the island, our feet frequently falling through the flimsy ceilings of the bird-burrows, our bodies obstructing the movements of shearwaters in flight, and of those alighting at or leaving the honeycomb of holes. We were hit several times by flying birds, we stepped on them, and we stumbled and fell over the rough pitted ground. The whole island, between midnight and three a.m., was one great bedlam of screaming and scuffling shearwaters. After three o'clock, at the first lightening of the north-east sky, the shearwaters began to dwindle, some vanishing down the holes, but the majority seemed to be taking off to sea. On the hilly rises of the ground, where there was a strong wind, they took off easily, but in the hollows they floundered along, their long wings making it difficult to get a purchase on the calm air, while their short legs, placed far back on the body, gave them insecure balance for running or walking or standing. In fact the shearwater cannot stand erect – it must lie flat on the breast when not in motion.

By four a.m., long before sunrise, not a live shearwater was to be seen on the island.

We were sleepy now, and glad of the sun's warmth to throw ourselves down in a sheltered hollow. When we woke the fishermen were waiting to take us back to what Mr Sturt called 'civilization'.

3

Skokholm at last
(1927)

Ronald Lockley landed on Skokholm for the first time at the beginning of June, 1927. Before leaving the mainland, Ronald had enjoyed a long conversation with an elderly man named Jack Edwards, from a mainland farm called Orlandon, who had lived with his wife on Skokholm for a while. The surname 'Edwards' was very common in Marloes at the time.

I find it difficult to tell you how wildly happy I was to be walking up those steps. From the conversation with Edwards of Orlandon and others, I had got enough information in the last two days to realise that I might with luck obtain this abandoned island for myself. I was astonished that no-one had snapped it up long ago. But here it was, waiting for me. My mind was already filled with the thoughts of a settler and pioneer as I put my foot on Skokholm for the first time.

On the sea and in the air were thousands of sea-birds. The cliffs were lavishly strewn with wildflowers, wide open to the sunlight. Rabbit-holes seemed to be discreetly draped with tresses of sea-campion, scurvy-grass, and lady's fingers, and at these decorated thresholds stood puffins, singly and in pairs. These small sea-birds have droll white faces. The parrot-like bill with its crimson, blue, and yellow rings is stuck on like a clown's artificial nose. The eye has a lead-coloured badge above and below, like the false eyelids of a clown, and the 'lips' are fleshy and pale orange in colour. The breast is white, like the face, but the rest of the plumage is black, including the cravat under the chin, but excepting a grey patch at the back of the head. The legs and feet are the colour of a blood-orange skin. The whole is like a toy alderman in evening-dress who has opened many crackers and adorned his face with the contents. Later in the year the puffin moults these adornments; even the yellow 'lips', or mouth flanges, disappear, as their purpose – that of attracting a mate or intimidating a rival, or both – is served.

We did not know then that the foundations of the farmhouse had probably been laid at least as long ago as the thirteenth century. But it had a pleasing air of great age in its lichen-covered and leaning walls, and though the roof had almost gone it seemed to invite assistance, to ask that it be lived in and cared for. We pushed our way past the hingeless doors of a roofless entrance porch into the principal room.

A rough driftwood bed stood upon a floor of rotten boards. Above, the floor of the loft made a ceiling, through holes in which we could see the sky and hear swallows at a nest in the rafters. The joists of the loft floor were hung with cobwebs, dried rabbit-skins, rags, and sacks. A large window was darkened by sacks stuffed into the many broken panes. We saw, when our eyes were focused to the dim light, some old cups, plates, and knives on a rough table. A mouse returned to nibble some scraps of bread lying there. A broken-down fireplace was full of wood ashes, and on the hearth a teapot with a broken spout squatted beside a large frying-pan with fat congealed in it. The shells of sea-birds' eggs were mingled with the hearth ashes.

A couple of sacks filled with hay served as a mattress, and a filthy greatcoat as a covering for the bed. Above this was fixed a shelf full of such lumber as worn-out rabbit-catching gear, tins, jars, rope, canvas, and a rusty muzzle-loader. Cobwebs covered the sooty paper and granulating plaster of the walls.

This place sheltered the fishermen from the mainland during the fine days of summer. It looked a regular hovel at first glance, but it was not long before I was satisfied that the house had its possibilities. The window of the main room looked east upon the sea and the mainland. Window, fireplace, and beams were well placed for an attractive living room.

There were other rooms entered by four small doors from the main room, but these were roofless, occupied by nesting blackbirds and wheatears, and hung with flowering rock spurrey and pennywort. On the east side was the garden, rank with bracken and bramble and walled with a bank of stone and earth, in which puffins and rabbits burrowed. To the north of the house the farm buildings were grouped, roofless, broken, and full of nettles and hogweed. Here nested hedge-sparrows and wagtails.

Larks sang, rabbits lay stretched out at the edge of the bluebells, their white bellies turned to the sun, wheatears bobbed at us, flicking their white rumps over the hedges, and a blackbird whistled from the direction of the spring at the bottom of the home meadow.

To sea westward the lonely hump of the islet of Grassholm rose green above the white overfalls of the Wild Goose Race. There was only a light air from the south, yet the race heaved violently as it ran counter to the breeze. North lay the rock-bound island of Skomer with its satellite, Midland, separated from the mainland by Jack Sound, through which we had sailed that morning. Eastward the mainland itself was a wall of high cliffs with strata upended as if cut with perpendicular blows from a giant chisel. One or two farms looked furtively over the edge of this barrier.

These farms and the lighthouse at St Ann's Head in the south-east were the only signs of human activity in our view.

Here, then, was space and peace to live in, and in the restoration of house and garden plenty of work of the kind a man might enjoy. As I glanced about me I was already planning a living out of what I saw. Surely a man could be content and self-supporting on this island, living on the produce of his garden, his fields, his nets and lines in the sea? For the rest, there would be the joy of breathing pure air, of watching birds and flowers, moods of sea and sky, of living free and independent. I was ready at that moment to begin the Crusoe life I had so long dreamed of living.

I walked in the garden, picturing in my mind's eye its appearance in a year's time. There would be a path from the gateway to the far end, and on each side of the walk there would be currant and gooseberry bushes with a border of some old favourites, such as sweet-william, stock, forget-me-not, nasturtium, and marigold. This would be a concession to sentiment rather than a desire for decoration, which would be out of place on this island already blazing with wildflowers. The rest of the garden would be given over entirely to vegetables. So I thought as I pushed a way through the wild growth, looking for the fruit bushes which Edwards of Orlandon had planted twenty years or so before. They had disappeared entirely, no doubt consumed by old age and by rabbits. A hedge-sparrow sang sweetly in one corner. A slow-worm glided from beneath some driftwood moved by my foot. A puffin came out of a hole in the wall and, surprised by my nearness, tumbled back into the bracken. I picked it up. It gave me a bite which drew blood. I threw it into the air, and it whirred away to the sea, but heavily, for its small wings are better adapted for swimming under water than flying in the air.

Ronald walked around Skokholm observing and noting the birdlife: guillemots, gulls, dunlins, choughs.

In this way, watching birds and cataloguing flowers, the hours darted past. Sun and wind had moved together all day, and now as the sun moved north-west over Grassholm the light breeze died, leaving the sea smooth and shining. Scarcely a ripple touched the foot of the cliffs. From time to time a seal breached the surface, showing the long hound-like profile of the grey or Atlantic species. It would stare at us for a moment, then with a snort, somersault downward, leaving a disk of foam behind it. Once a school of porpoises steamed past, rising and blowing with the timed energy of a ship's piston-rods.

A pair of choughs, or red-billed crows – rare enough in England today – had a nest in the crevice in the high cliffs which crown the extreme south-west point of the island.

I had nearly forgotten that there was a lighthouse on the island. I should not be entirely cut off from other human beings after all. The lighthouse stood right on the headland. The three keepers were glad enough to see fresh faces, and we had a cup of tea with them in their warm kitchen. Their well-built, almost hotel-like lighthouse is a mile from the old farmhouse and the landing-place in South Haven. A light tram-line connects the lighthouse and the landing, and the trucks, they said, were drawn by a donkey known to the lightkeepers as Edward Edwards – because it came from Marloes.

When we got back to the farmhouse the two fishermen who had brought us to the island that morning were getting supper. They were frying thick rashers of bacon over a driftwood fire in the hearth. On the table was a lobster with the steam of cooking still rising from it, and beside this an old family Bible opened at a page in Job. When he could not talk, said the thin Fisherman John, he liked to read. This old Bible was dated 1763.

The fishermen had had a good day at the lobster-pots in the lee of Skokholm, and were now tired and hungry. They shared their meal with us – first lobster, then fried gulls' eggs. That first gulls' egg I had ever tasted seemed to me more sweet and delicate than a pullet's egg. We ate the last eggs in the house, and had to collect a fresh supply. The fisherman led the way across the plateau. In every gull's nest with three eggs they placed their heels. One and two eggs in a nest were collected.

"The murdering thieves'll lay us a fresh clutch if we smash these," said John. "They'll lay twice in the same nest, but for the third clutch they'll deceive you by laying in a new place."

We reached Mad Bay. Away to sea a great shadow lay on the water. "Them's the cuckles waiting for the night to fall before they come ashore to their nests in the rabbit-holes," said John. The carpet of birds, half a mile long, rose and wheeled, and then settled again. It did this several times, as if the shearwaters – for that is the proper name of the 'cuckles' – were impatient for night to come.

My heart was torn to see the fishermen now filling their caps with the eggs of the razorbills, which they said were the most delicious of all, for I had begun to admire these birds and their pleasant manners. John said that they would lay again, but he spoke glibly and unconvincingly.

The sun had set behind a tent of dark cloud. Back in the house we lit candles and prepared to sleep on the floor. The candles guttered and went out, leaving the room with a glow from the wood fire.

Suddenly there was a loud scream overhead, a sobbing "Ooh-ooh-aah!"

We sprang up. John jumped nervously out of bed,

recovered himself, stretched and yawned, then threw another log on the fire. But Jack snored on unheeding. The sobbing notes outside increased.

'The cuckles is in,' said John, warming his thin hands by the flame. 'You'd best get out and enjoy 'em, for it's only on a dark night like this that you'll hear 'em at all.'

We went outside. The raft of 'cuckles' had left the gathering place on the sea, and the birds were coming home to their burrows in twos and threes, dozens and scores. Each bird seemed to try to outscream the last. Imagine a pair of cocks crowing out of tune, and their heads being suddenly cut off near the end of the discordant duet. That is what the call of the shearwater is like. Yet no two calls are the same.

Out in the meadow they glided unseen about us, brushing past, even crashing into us, while from underground their mates, incubating the one egg deep in a rabbit-burrow, answered them with muffled crowing. The torch showed many shearwaters sitting on the ground at the entrances to the burrows, singly or in pairs, but these birds were dazed by the light, and refused to continue their natural business. They wriggled and bit furiously when picked up.

The shearwater's wings are long and narrow, adapted for gliding low over the waves. On land these wings are a handicap, as they do not permit an easy take-off. Nor do the feet help; these are placed so far to the rear of the body that the breast falls forward to the ground. The shearwater blunders along on all fours, so to speak, and it needs a fresh wind to enable it to get clear of the rough ground. That calm night many simply scrambled along until they reached the seaward slope. There they launched easily into the air and vanished in the darkness over the sea.

The screaming of the shearwaters became a regular bedlam soon after midnight. It did not prevent our hearing the sweeter, softer crooning notes of the storm-petrels, which were nesting here and there in the old hedge-walls, in the screeds of the cliffs, and under boulders and stones. 'Purr-rr-chikka! Purr-rr-chikka!' they crooned, and the torch, flashed into the crannies between the stones, showed this swallow-like bird brooding its one white egg. This Mother Carey's chicken of the sailor, foreteller of storm at sea, is a small sooty-black bird. Even the fine legs and webbed feet are black, but the rump is pure white, and there is a smear of white under the wing. One came unintentionally to my hand as I lay with my ear to a crevice. Discovering its mistake, it opened its mouth and spat forth a shower of amber-coloured fluid. The warm oily stuff dripping from my hand smelt no worse than musk. It was probably digested plankton, gathered at sea, which one bird would give to the other at the nest. I told the bird it was a wicked imp, and I let it go after I had turned it over in my hand and marvelled that such a frail-looking thing could withstand the great gales which sweep the North Atlantic Ocean in the winter. The storm-petrel is no bigger really than a large sparrow.

It was growing light as we moved home across the bluebells and the bracken. There was a slight dew. The clouds rolled slowly away from the bright east, like shutters raised at daybreak. The last shearwaters called and were gone either down their holes or off to sea. The storm-petrels danced for the last time – we could dimly see them over their nesting crannies – then they vanished. The crooning from the stones ceased.

A puffin came out of its hole, yawned like a sleepy child, flapped its wings, then, seeing us, hastily dived back to earth. In the thicket by the spring the sedge-warbler rattled a few notes, challenging our passing as it had challenged the shearwaters all night, for the little brown bird will let no noise or movement pass without a word or two of scolding, and will lose its sleep in consequence on this island of noisy nights.

Next to sing was the wheatear. Its jumbled notes were answered by the hedge-sparrows and pipits round the house. Before the sun appeared above the mainland in the east the blackbird rolled out its round notes: 'Who told you so? I told you so!' The gulls took up their harsh mewing. The island day, just begun, had ended for us. We dragged our rugs into the sunlight and lay down to sleep in its warmth.

4

Alice, Doris and Ann
(1927–1930)

When Ronald returned to Cardiff he began negotiations to become tenant of Skokholm. At last he secured the legal right to dwell in 'the peaceful possession and quiet enjoyment' *of the island. When he told some old friends from Cardiff about Skokholm, they were a little sceptical. But the daughter of the family, Doris, responded with envy and enthusiasm – so much so, said Ronald, that he* 'renounced celibacy' *from that day – 12 July 1927 – and promised Doris he would marry her one year hence, when he had made Skokholm ready for her. In August 1927 she and her father and other relatives visited the island with Ronald.*

It was a calm day, and we took two hours to cross with oars only. As we drew near the red cliffs of Dream Island we put out lines to catch our suppers, and were rewarded with both mackerel and pollack.

It was now early August, and the cliff-nesting birds, the guillemots and razorbills, had left, but there were still many puffins, gulls and oyster-catchers, and some small land-loving birds. The puffins were busy feeding their nearly fledged young, and all that afternoon could be seen bringing sprats to the nesting holes. With the aid of our glasses we could see that Mr. Puffin held three or more sprats in his beak, heads to one side, and tails to the other. Now how does he manage to arrange them so neatly? And how does he catch more than one at a time? We saw a lazy herring-gull watching the incoming puffins, now and then swooping down on a bird just about to enter its hole. The puffin would then hastily drop his sprats, which the robber calmly swallowed.

Over the ruined island dwelling five buzzards were soaring. Up and up they soared, wheeling round and round without a flap of their broad wings until they were almost lost in the blue sky. We found later that the buzzards had come for a nefarious purpose: to slaughter the young birds and young rabbits, and to kill any defenceless shearwater which had lost its way or been unable to rise from the bracken overnight.

The visitors were impressed by the lovely colours of the island: the red rocks, lichened in pale green here and there, the purple heather now in flower. Only campion, of the spring flowers, remained in bloom, but there were stretches of golden-rod, ragwort, variegated wild pansies and birdsfoot trefoil.

The gloom and filth of the interior of the old house did not dismay Doris so much as it did her three companions. She boldly cooked the fish in the ancient frying-pan and put good heart into all by feeding us well.

There and then she gave me directions for reconstructing the old dwelling to her liking. They were simple enough. I was to remove the partition between living-room and ante-room, thus making one large room; to remove the wall between the little kitchen and the little room on the south side, this making for her a reasonably large kitchen, where she might carry on in comfort the cooking and baking which would be inseparable from such an isolated home. This, and a roof for her head, was all she asked of me, and she demanded that I should leave as much pioneer work as possible undone that she might eventually share therein.

That evening the living-room was looking trimmer than it had been for many years. The cobwebs were swept away, and a roaring driftwood fire built up.

Early in the morning we came in from a long overnight inspection of the shearwaters and the storm-petrels, and ate our supper-cum-breakfast of fish, toast and tea with hearty appetite.

The storm-petrels we found flying like swallows everywhere on the island at night, but especially about the South Haven. Several pairs were nesting in a heap of limestones above the old lime-kiln, and we could hear the newly hatched chicks uttering a very plaintive 'Peep-peep'. We uncovered one nest and found both parents tending their solitary, young downy chick. The petrels were nesting, too, in cracks and chinks in the hedge-walls, and there was even a nestling in a crack in the outside wall of the dwelling house. These airy little birds, by day restless wanderers on the sea, at night could be seen, though dimly, flying with a quick, swallow-like grace, perfectly at home, about and over the rocks and walls where they had their young.

A strong wind came with sunrise. The fishermen, who had moored the boat in South Haven overnight, hastened to the house to say that it was time to go. Before we could make ready, however, quite a stiff wind was blowing directly into the little haven.

The waves began to rise and roar in and about it.

The fishermen leaped agilely into their boat, which was straining and tossing wildly at its moorings. We were invited to leap after them – from the landing steps. It was an exciting moment, but at last everyone had leaped or tumbled aboard without serious mishap. Fortunately the three lightkeepers, with whom we had made good friends, had come down from the lighthouse to see us off, and they held the mooring-ropes so as to assist us and to pull the boat away from the steps. They waved us good-bye, and watched us sail away swiftly before the rising summer gale.

Ronald then set about repairing the old barn, so as to be able to live in it while dealing with the old house, which he planned to start in the spring of 1928.

By Christmas-time I had repaired the roof and walls of the barn. For mortar we dug a fine earthy sandpit under an outcrop of rock in the middle of the island. This earthy sand, mixed with equal parts of lime and of ashes (from the large, ancient midden near the farmhouse door), made a very cheap, strong mortar. With patience and practice I learned to build up the gaps in the walls first, and then, encouraged, went on to repair the roof. New rafters and plates were necessary in one place and here the driftwood timber was employed. I put in for a wall-plate a solid oak plank which should last at least a century. Laths were laid across the rafters, and I next gathered the fallen tiles and sorted them to their sizes, the largest at the eaves and smallest at the ridge. Each tile had to have a wooden peg to hang on to the laths by, and a bed of mortar to rest upon above the preceding row. It became a fascinating, if slow, task. But I was pleased because everything except the lime was produced on the island. Even the tiles had been dug from the little quarry on the island many years ago; they were irregular, thick and heavy, but of a pleasant, yellowy grey colour.

About this time Ronald built a wooden hut on the mainland at Martinshaven, two miles from Marloes, so that he had somewhere to stay if rough seas made crossing to the island impossible.

Then, on Skokholm in late February 1928 Ronald discovered something that was going to be invaluable to him for several years.

One morning I strolled out of doors, early and eager to work, there to find, fast in the rocky cliff below tall Spy Rock, a fine old wooden schooner with all her sails spread to the now gentle south-east breeze! There had been a strong wind all night, accompanied by heavy must, and now here she was – a wonderful prize.

When you have lived long enough (it need not be very long!) on a sea-coast, everything that the sea gives up you grow greedy to take. You even dream of a great ship crushed on the beach, pouring out its life-blood of innumerable spars and canvas, tools and treasure, which you will be greedy to fight for, steal, and hide from the sight of preventive officers. You think rather less of the possible loss of life than of the spoils of the wreck. In short, a wreck proves to you how avaricious you really are. I believe my first thoughts when I saw the schooner were as discreditable as any confirmed beachcomber's.

Looking directly down upon the schooner from the high cliff above I was able to admire and to pity her to my heart's content. The tops of her topmasts were on a level with me. Her two large sails, the main and fore, were all set, as were her two topsails, the upper and lower, on the foremast. Her bowsprit, in striking the cliffs, had broken off short, the stump leaning out over the lower cliff in such a way as to form a convenient gangway for agile persons. The jibsails, or headsails, were torn to shreds, which hung in the stay-wires of the broken bowsprit. The ship itself was quite fast in a cleft in the cliff. She had evidently blown in at high water, ramming her stern against the sheer cliff on one side, and her bow against the shelving rocks of the other side.

The decks were in confusion when John and I boarded her. Ropes and chains were strewn everywhere, but there was no sign of life aboard. A peep into the hold revealed the cargo. Instead of gold and silver ingots, the hold was full of black diamonds – coal! There must have been two hundred tons of coal on board the good old *Alice Williams,* for that was her name, painted and carved on bow and stern.

Then quite suddenly I saw amid the wreckage a woman's face – a strong, bright face with piercing blue eyes that gazed far-seeing into the blue sky. The woman still wore her hair neatly coiled, with a black ribbon and red roses still twined in it. She also wore a white frock with an old-fashioned tight bodice, and around her neck was a rosary of jet and a black cross that matched her raven hair. She floated serenely on the water, despite the fact that one of her arms was missing.

'Quick, John,' I cried – 'a rope here, boy!'

Again and again we threw a rope with a hook on the end down to the floating lady. She took not the slightest notice of our frantic efforts for her rescue. At last the grapple caught in a coil of her hair and without any ceremony we hauled her up bodily over the ship's rail. It was Alice Williams herself, the serene and proud figure-head of the schooner, dressed, as she was first conceived, in the fashion of the eighteen-fifties. True to her ship she had stayed to the last, even when struck off by the rocks, and when all the others had abandoned it.

We propped her up beside the ship's wheel on the poop, and I then paced the decks wondering what to do with this prize ship. Would she move out of her rocky berth? I could but try.

'Stand by there, John, my lad!' I bellowed, taking the wheel from Alice. 'Cut anchors and hoist the flying jib; we'll away to London Town and sell this good ship for a thousand golden doubloons!'

'Aye, aye, sir!' cried John, who in his day had served on more than one schooner and ketch. 'Hey there, bos'n, fetch the crew and step lively to it! Up aloft wi' ye and shake out the foretop skysails!'

The gulls laughed back at us, and the high cliff echoed, but the ship never moved. She was in her last haven. Her wooden sides and keel had settled once and for all in the cradle of red island boulders. The wheel-shaft had broken off near the rudder-post, and there was a hole in her bows from which coal already leaked.

'Ye'd best make the most of her, sir', said John. 'In a day of wind she'll be swept to the bottom.'

'Tis plunder, then, John,' I said. We'll save what we can.'

Below deck, as the tide ebbed, we found the cabin, fo'c'sle, and sail-room in great disorder and full of broken panelling, planks and timer. The captain's instruments, the ship's china and kitchenware were washed away already, but I saw my opportunity to lay in a stock of coal to last me for many years. It remained to get together enough hands to work the cargo out of the hold and on to the ledges of the cliff – no easy task, I was to find.

That day John and I lowered the brand-new mainsail and the old red foresail and cut them from the bolt-ropes. On the end of the lower topsail-yard, which leaned out towards the cliff, we fixed a block, and through it reeved a rope to the ships winch. John turned the winch while I fastened the sails one at a time on to the rope. Up and up soared the folded mainsail until it touched the block on the end of the yard and, hanging thus over the cliff and the ship, could go no higher. Then I climbed ashore, and as John lowered the rope slowly pulled the great heavy canvas down on to the cliff. In this way the foresail was hoisted ashore, and finally Alice Williams herself was tenderly swung up to the yard and down to the cliff. There I leaned her against the rocks in such a position that she could watch all subsequent proceedings on her wrecked ship.

The next day Ronald went ashore to Marloes to pick up Henry, a sixteen-year-old who had worked for him on his farm in Cardiff, who was going to help out on the island. While on the mainland Ronald phoned the local ships' underwriter in order to legalise his salvage operations.

From the underwriter I learned that the *Alice Williams* had got out of control in the night, her headsails having been carried away by the half-gale, and, as she was in danger of drifting on to the rocks in this unmanageable state, anchors were dropped. These, however, dragged, so, after sending up distress flares, the crew of five finally lowered the ship's boat and abandoned the schooner. They were later picked up a trawler near St. Ann's and taken to Milford Haven.

I bought the good ship *Alice Williams* over the phone for the sum of £5, anchors and chains not included.

Before leaving the mainland Ronald pulled together a gang of six volunteers to help with the salvage operations: Henry and John; a mason whom Ronald had been trying vainly to induce to the island to help with the house repairs (Ronald promised him a boatload of coal for his services);and a Captain Cristal, with Billy, a jobbing labourer.

When all the newcomers had admired the wreck and trod the decks till the novelty of doing so had worn off, we set to work, and carried on merrily for several days. John and the mason wound the winch which hoisted the coal out of the hold by the basket-load. Cristal and Billy loaded the baskets, while I pulled them in to the cliff and piled the coal on the ledges. It was very heavy, hard work. On the third day Cristal missed his footing on the deck and fell into the hold. Luckily the tide had just begun to fill the ship, so that he had nothing more hurtful than a swim in dirty water, but, until he emerged, black and wet, we were mystified by his sudden and complete disappearance. Even this fall did not damp his merry spirits, which were at all times the life of this strangely assorted crew.

Henry, a delighted grin perpetually on his fresh young face, helped, in between his duties as head cook and bottle-washer. When we were thirsty between meals he brought us an enormous kettle (ex *Alice Williams*) of tea. He was detailed to get our supper, which consisted of a saucepan or two full of boiled potatoes, swedes and salt beef ('ship's junk' from the pickle-chest of the *Alice Williams*) – a simple enough supper, but one to which our ravenous appetites did full justice. After supper in the old house the six of us would gather before a roaring fire of new coal from the wreck, and yarns flew around until midnight. When we were all too tired to talk we fell asleep.

The next day's work began somewhere about sunrise, and went on until sunset.

The sea, at high water, was on a level with the schooner's deck, and it was not possible to work then for an hour or two, so we spent this period in hauling the coal, sails, rope and gear already ashore on to higher ground, using my handwinch, which was mounted on the top of the cliff.

Each tide had its effect on the *Alice Williams*, working and prising loose more and more of her planking. Soon the keel was pressing up through the ship, each day lifting the masts a few inches higher above the sinking deck. At high-water the whole ship rocked gently to and fro, the masts swaying and creaking ominously. The first breeze or ground-swell must inevitably bring her total dissolution. Therefore, we toiled each day until we were worn out, trying to save the coal that at each tide leaked by the ton out of the rent in the bows. But after four days' work we had piled up enough coal, I hoped, to last me many years.

At the end of six days most of the coal had been washed out of the hold, and the old schooner was tilted at a sharp angle, awaiting her end. The masts were askew and only held in place by the stout rigging. I believe there were tears in Alice's eyes, but to spare her the final agonies I carried her up to the top of Spy Rock beside the island flagpole. Here she might still breast a salty wind and look out over restless seas, with foam and white water below her.

It was now getting too risky to work on board. The neap tides did not entirely leave the schooner by day. Moreover, my crew were thoroughly exhausted, ready to give up and depart to civilisation once more. Se we put them ashore, with due thanks for their voluntary services.

Two days later there came a half gale from south-east and the *Alice Williams* was totally destroyed. The wind and sea piled her fragments high on the island beaches. I was able to select all and more than I wanted of oak beams and other timber for the reconstruction of my future home.

With March birds flocked in still greater numbers to the island, the early spring arrivals mingling with the winter visitors. In the middle of the month the wheatears arrived, dozens of them flying low about the stone hedge-walls, bobbing, curtseying and calling, 'Jack, Jack' to me. The lesser black-backed gulls came quite suddenly to occupy the island bog. They sat together in pairs on the long grass, and resented with loud cries the approach of any human form. The ravens had long built their nest on the cliff in Mad Bay, and now had a ravenous young brood of five to feed. They had built a strong nest of dead heather-stems and roots, and had lined it warmly with fibres and rabbits' wool. Late in the month came the chiffchaff, and flights of starlings, rooks and chaffinches – all transitory visitors, hurrying in some northerly direction to their breeding haunts.

Primroses were at their best, growing in the bays and on the slopes of the island cliffs. South Haven was yellow with primroses and lesser celandines. Sea campion and violets were just beginning to flower.

While we were occupied in building the barn my thoughts turned much on the future. This first year I would not have time to be a fisherman; the summer would pass all too quickly in house-building. Yet it was all very well to build a home and then not have the means to support one. I therefore planned out my slender capital as carefully as I could. In the future my income must come from the products of the island: from rabbits, fish, and the future farm. To produce most of my foodstuffs was the ideal to aim at, and to achieve as much independence as possible. The garden must be a large one. I must keep goats for milk and hens for eggs. Later I would be a shepherd as well, with a large flock of sheep to give both pleasure and profit.

The garden had already been deeply dug over, and now waited to be set. Doris intended to put in the garden seeds herself, but I was not sure that I wanted her to come just yet, and to find nothing accomplished in house-restoration.

We worked feverishly at the barn. Henry took entire charge of the culinary and house-cleaning operations in the old dwelling. I taught him how to make bread and to cook generally, and he was soon adding flourishes of his own to the art. He read recipes secretly and brought some amazing, but mostly palatable, dishes to the table. The fare was simple enough. Fried bread and bacon for breakfast; vegetables, most swedes and potatoes, for dinner, with bully beef or tinned meat of some kind; for tea, toast, butter and ham, and on Sundays any cake Henry thought fit to surprise us with. At each meal mugs of tea helped to allay a thirst obtained by hard work. Just before bedtime, cocoa and toast was to be had by anyone who liked to get it himself. Sundays were holidays. Once a week, and sometimes once only in a fortnight, did we cross to the mainland for letters and more building materials.

We had an excellent supply of oak from the wreck for lintels and beams. The brass-bound wheel of the schooner we fixed in the breast of the chimney-piece we had built in the barn. When this wheel was duly polished until the wood and brass shone it was quite a resplendent sight under the lofty beams of this large room. Moreover, it was not to be a mere ornament. If one seized the spokes and swung the wheel four turns to starboard a chain came sliding down the chimney. It was an easy matter then to hook the kettle on for tea. When the kettle boiled, four turns of the wheel to port raised it off the fire. This was the great trick to play on visitors. Nonchalantly Henry would swing the great wheel; and be delighted to see the stranger mystified by the movement of the kettle.

Early in April the barn was as far renovated as I intended it to be for the present, and we moved in wholesale from the house. My few items of furniture were easily accommodated in the new premises. We laid the great red foresail of the schooner over the floor, which was composed of wide, flat slabs of red island stone. The ship's tattered flags, her lifebuoys and some panelling, decorated and made bright the whitewashed walls. Opposite the wheel and chimney, at the other end of the room, we fixed the heavy, carved timber, decorated in white and black check, which once accompanied Alice on the schooner's bow. Above it, in the high apex window, the ship's binnacle and compass rested; to port and starboard respectively, in the corners of this end of the room, hung the ship's red port lamp and her green starboard one. Outside the door the ship's fog-bell served as a musical knocker for visitors and a summons-bell for meals, whilst her carved name-plate, torn from her bow by the sea, had been rescued and was now nailed forever on a conspicuous lower beam inside.

In this picturesque den we lived while we were repairing the dwelling-house. We slept each on his own ship's cot, rescued from the wreck and newly sewn over with red sail canvas; and very comfortably we slept too. Barn was a much too prosaic name for this living-room, dominated by the dazzling brightness of the brass on the wheel, which Henry was under strict orders to keep shining. So henceforth it was called the 'Wheelhouse'.

In April, Doris arrived on the island with her father, who was known as 'Admiral', to see what progress had been made on the house.

We had whitewashed and decorated the one habitable little room in the old house for the distinguished lady visitor. For the first time also the table was spread in state in the Wheelhouse, a genuine tablecloth and china making a spotless display such as the old place had never known before. This, with a roaring fire of wreck coal and wood, was to welcome and warm the visitors after their cold voyage over a wind-whipped sea.

Zealously did Doris sow the garden with beans, peas, carrots, parsnips, and plant greens, rhubarb, shallots, currants and gooseberries, while I laid in the potato rows. Admiral, with his expert mastery of the joiner's craft, was not idle either. Together the three of us demolished the partition between the house-kitchen and the roofless room beside it, in order to work the will of Doris to have a larger kitchen. This partition proved to be nearly three feet thick and contained a chimney and fireplace which had been walled in at some time long past. The result was that, when all the stones and mortar had been removed, Doris had a long, low-roofed kitchen for her delight, facing southwards to the shelter of the hill.

Then Doris was gone again, to return after the wedding in July. Life got back to normal on Skokholm.

The puffins had returned late in March to the Sounds, and there was great excitement on the 3rd of April, when they finally made up their minds to land. This they did very suddenly and thoroughly at midday, flying inland by the hundred and occupying all their favourite positions on the high points, the rock outcrops and the stony hedge-walls. There they jigged and bowed and laughed sonorously in their usual manner, for three hours, before flying away altogether. Two days later they again made a landing in force, and, as before, disappearing after a few hours. A bitter north-east wind, on April 16th, had the effect of driving them entirely away from the sea near the island, but they returned in thousands on the 18th, and the next day landed for the season.

The shearwaters, of course, had been here since February, and were now about to lay their solitary white egg in the recess at the end of a rabbit-burrow. The storm-petrels had only begun to arrive at night in the last few days of April. April and May were, indeed, wonderful months for one who loved birds. Each day saw new visitors, quickly come and quickly gone. After the wheatears and chiffchaffs came the swallows and sand-martins. Every day throughout April, May and early June swallows passed over the meadows, sometimes in hundreds, but more often by twos and threes, steadily from dawn till dusk. Then came willow-wrens, swarming in the newly-grown nettles and bramble-bushes, olivaceous-coloured birds difficult to distinguish from the chiffchaffs at a distance, except when, at rare intervals, they paused to utter a few bars of song. But all these migrants were, as a rule, too restless and busy seeking food to have inclination to sing.

White wagtails on their way north, probably to Iceland and the Faroes, visited the island from March to mid-April, generally in small flocks of from a dozen to fifty. They came freely about the garden and buildings, causing a certain excitement to the pair of pied wagtails, their close relations, which had built a nest in an old wall near the Wheelhouse.

A few cuckoos called over the island, but were soon gone. Whitethroats were plentiful on some days, and late in April came the sleek, brown sedge-warblers, swarming in the nettles as did the willow-wrens. One pair remained to nest in the thicket of hemlock dropwort at the foot of the home meadow, where a spring runs down from the well. The male bird was the sweetest songster we had on the island that summer, and after singing all day would begin again at night as soon as the first incoming shearwater's cry disturbed his fitful sleep.

A few swifts, a few house-martins, and many whinchats completed the list of April migrants. With May came spotted flycatchers, grasshopper-warblers and turtle-doves. Of larger birds there were occasional rooks, daws, common sand-pipers and whimbrel, besides quite a long list of birds of which only one or two of its kind were noted.

One day a very handsome and distinguished visitor settled on the bank in front of the window. It was a hoopoe, a brilliantly coloured bird not unlike a small jay, with a sulphur-tipped, fan-shaped head-crest which it erected for a moment as it settled on the hedge-bank. The hoopoe is a rare British bird, and this pretty fellow did not stay with us longer than one day. It flew about the island with that rising and falling method of flight, wings now closed and now wide-spread, adopted by woodpeckers.

Ronald and John started work on the dwelling-house. A lot of the timbers salvaged from the Alice Williams *were used, one of them replacing an old lintel which had been salvaged from another ship, perhaps four hundred years old.*

The guest-room was refloored with flooring boards laid over joists consisting of the thick deck-planks of the *Alice Williams*. The main room, when the ante-room partition had been knocked down and a new floor put across the timbers of the loft overhead, made an attractively large living-room. The long, oak beaks, cleaned of ages of dirt, were still straight and strong, so that we were saved the trouble of tearing the walls down to renew them. For a stairway to the loft we had the step-ladder from the cabin of the wreck. The handrail from the schooner, too, when trimmed to required lengths, furnished me with the framing of the fireplace, which I had made rather spacious for burning logs and driftwood.

Alice Williams, you will see, had been most useful, saving much expense of material and the labour of ferrying it over. She had furnished me with timbers of such quality as I should scarcely have been able to afford. Nor do I forget that, apart from the house-building, there were other directions in which she had been most useful. There were, for instance, innumerable items of use in boating, such as canvas, rope, wire, blocks, chains, tools, etc. Her fresh-water tank, capable of holding 200 gallons, we set up for catching and storing precious rain-water from the house-roof. The cook's galley we rolled laboriously across the meadows into one of the farm folds, and there I set it up to serve as a fowl-house when the hens arrived. The other deck-house was also rolled into a convenient place near the house.

July arrived, and found me putting the last touches to the interior of the home I had promised Doris, though there was much to be done still to the outside; a lot of pioneering still left for her to take part in.

July the twelfth proved a day of sunshine after many days of uncertain weather and mist. There was a slight breeze from the south-east, so that I was able to sail quietly northwards from the island, and across St. Bride's Bay to St. Bride's Haven. Here, within a stone's throw of the church, anchor was dropped and I went ashore to meet my bride.

When the ceremony was over, shortly after noon, our parents and sisters, almost the sole witnesses of our quiet wedding, drank our health at the feast held on the edge of the grass, after which we were free to sail away alone together. It was almost the first time I had handled the boat without John, but I was proud to be able to sail away in the bright, newly-painted *Storm-Petrel* with my bride. Proudly did the infant engine start us on our way, and then, when I hoisted sail, we sped away out into St. Bridge's Bay with a hissing wake of white foam behind us.

First of all Doris must needs view the home built for her, and to this end we sailed down for the island. But when we had passed through Jack Sound we met a heavy mist rolling up from the Atlantic. Some farmers, aware of the wedding, had assembled on the cliff near Jack Sound and now fired us a salute from their double-barrels, and just before the mist enveloped us entirely.

Ann came after the lambs in May [1930]. Convenience dictated that she should be born on the mainland. Three weeks later I came over to fetch her and her mother. The *Storm-Petrel,* shining with a new coat of paint, flew a pennon at bow and masthead. The day was calm, with hot sunshine struggling to dispel the morning vapour. A thousand bright-winged birds fluttered over the still sea, diving, swimming and fishing among the ripples of our wake. When we drew in towards the island harbour we were pleased to see it festooned with bunting. The flags spelt out a gay W-E-L-C-O-M-E in the International Code. The lightkeepers stood to salute us, and a cheer was raised as eager hands lifted the Princess's cradle ashore. Punch the pony was there, harnessed to carry her, still sleeping from the rocking of the boat, up to the house, above which the three code flags spelling her name stirred gently in the windless air. Our flagstaff had been made into a Maypole, and later, when the mist cleared, all the flags danced to the tune of the north wind in the stay-wires.

The first time we voyaged with Ann the wicker cradle fitted nicely into the cockpit where the old engine used to be. In the early days the movement of the boat nearly always sent her to sleep, but at times her eyes would be open and would be attracted by the kittiwake which often settled on the truck of the mast, or by the sweep of a gull passing overhead. A year later her little hands would be raised towards the bird, and the note of her perpetual wonder became 'Look! Look!' Now that she is able to dispense with the cradle she sits and points out the birds to us, her eyes sometimes keener than ours. When the sea is calm she walks about with enthusiasm, steadying herself with her small legs to match the angle of the swaying boat; only in tide-races and white wind-whipped water must she have the protection of someone's arms.

The sea greatly fascinates her, and it became in the first days a problem to circumvent her growing determination to study it from the landing-steps in South Haven. But seeing me carrying a strayed sheep up a steep cliff one day she became anxious for my safety, and so learned to value hers.

5

Grassholm and Bardsey

(1928–1930)

Ronald Lockley wrote not just about the island he knew best, Skokholm, but other islands, off Wales and elsewhere. In his books he used and 'amplified' material which had appeared as articles in The Countryman *magazine over the years. These are extracts from those chapters.*

As soon as he arrived on Skokholm Ronald had wanted to explore nearby Grassholm, but he had promised his future wife Doris that she could go with him on the first expedition. Soon after Doris had settled into the farmhouse, and on a fine day, they set off.

Grassholm

We had made such good progress that I had no more fear of currents. I screwed shut the throttle of the engine, and we covered the last few miles under sail. The east side of the small pyramid of Grassholm was green as a spring meadow, with no sign of the thousands of nesting gannets. But as soon as we were within half a mile several hundreds of these great white birds suddenly flew out to inspect us. Many leaden bills and pale fishy eyes were turned down to look at us as they skimmed past. They wheeled silently, then in a body returned to the island. This reconnoitre and escorting manoeuvre was one which we were to observe on many occasions when reaching or leaving Grassholm.

From lack of knowledge of the rocky shore we entered the south instead of the south-east gut, where the fishermen usually moored their boats. But it was dead calm in the lee here, and we had no trouble in throwing a line across the creek and mooring the boat. Kittiwakes and the herring-gulls and great black-backed gulls were overhead. Four or five grey seals made way for us on the sloping rocks where they had been lolling dry in the sun. They rolled like ninepins into the water, dived, then swam close in behind us, nostrils and eyes working as they tried to discover whether friend or foe had disturbed them. A dozen more, hidden somewhere in the rocks, were moaning a wild kind of dirge. We threw our food, water, and blankets ashore and scrambled along to watch them.

There they were, taking their ease on the weed-covered rock just below the high-water mark, stretched in every kind of attitude, some with their heads lower than their tails, some on their backs, some on their bellies. There was one fine black seal, by his length of nine or ten feet probably a bull. Alongside him was one just as big, but cream-coloured and even whiter on one side where his pale fur had dried out in the sun before he rolled half over. He was asleep. But the velvet one and the rest – a nondescript bunch of mottled greys and browns – had not yet settled down. They were like a lot of old people who had come ashore after a bathe. They were rubbing, rolling into comfortable positions, scratching head and body with their well-clawed fore-flippers, yawning freely, and now and then giving out a musical moan.

Here and there one dozed off as we watched. Two or three more came out of the sea and threw their great bodies on the rocks, hunching along like overfed caterpillars. These were greeted by the rest with renewed lamentations. It seemed to me that those in possession were warning the new arrivals to keep off the particular sun-parlours already occupied. The skins of the seals looked drum-tight. No doubt they were full as well as sleepy.

Ronald and Doris then struggled across Grassholm to the highest rock of the island. Progress was difficult because they had to negotiate a large expanse of land which had been burrowed into, and undermined, by puffins – only a handful were left on the island in 1928. Finally they reached the vantage point.

From this point the gannets are spread below you like some rare ballet in blue and silver and gold.

It is impossible for me to describe as it deserves to be described, that sight of ten thousand or so big white birds spaced so closely and evenly over two acres of sloping ground. Each bird, or pair of birds, was guarding a hummock crowned with a nest of seaweed and dead grass, and each bird was as beautiful to look at as the whole colony itself, the white head tinged with golden yellow, the bill plumbous and bayonet-like, the eye pale as silver, the plumage snow-white except for the black wing-tips, and the legs and the toes of the webbed feet black with unreal longitudinal stripes of blue-green. In each nest was a single young bird, a ball of white down from which protruded black beak and feet. Here and there was an unhatched egg or a youngster with the black juvenile feathers well grown. Overhead was a great wheel of thousands of gannets moving steadily northward over the colony, then turning southward over the sea to complete the circle. The wing-spread of a gannet must be nearly six feet. The great squadron sailed close over our heads, each individual glancing down at us with those cold but human-looking eyes, with golden head bent and bill pointed at us.

Some years later we were to make a film of this Grassholm gannetry.

We now had our notebooks out. There was no difficulty in cataloguing the plants. There were only two grasses: the sweet sheep's fescue and the sour fog grass. A few sea-mallows, chickweed, Atriplex, English stonecrop, sea-pinks, rock spurrey, and scurvy-grass completed the list. Of birds, rock-pipits sang in every creek, and one had a nest on the grassy top of the island. Oyster-catchers claimed the bare rocks above the tide-line, and guillemots and razor-bills nested in haphazard fashion, often in accessible situations – some even in the centre of the gannetry, where they passed to and fro without comment from the gannets. Kittiwakes, usually associated with steep ledges, had built their nests on little rock shelves inland in places I could reach by hand. They were very tame. It was clear that today very few people came to disturb the islet, and the worst enemies of the other birds were probably those robbers, the great black-backed gull and the herring gull. These gulls had well-grown young scrambling about the island; like ostriches, the brown chicks buried their heads in holes and burrows when we passed by.

From the top of the island we saw the sun set beyond the Smalls reef, a chain of low rocks six miles to the west, on one of which is perched a tall light-house banded in red and white.

There was a fine-weather promise in the rosy look of the sky. The wind fell very light. The gannets settled down for the night, their rattle, like that of a hay-cutting machine, which had been going on all day, subsided, and the last birds flew out from the colony. One adult gannet remained to guard each chick. The silence seemed strange.

The boat was motionless in that south creek, from which the wide sea stretched away to the coast of Brazil, a few thousand miles away. We made a bed in the grass under blankets. I wondered if there were petrels – storm-petrels and possibly Leach's fork-tailed petrels – breeding on this remote island. But if there were petrels or shearwaters we did not hear them, though we listened from a time as the moon rose full and clear above the shadowy outline of our island of Skokholm away in the east.

Bardsey

A few years later, while Doris and Ann went to stay with relations for a while, Ronald decided to go and visit Bardsey Island (Ynys Enlli), off south-west Gwynedd – then Caernarvonshire. He wished to visit other 'small islands with people on them', and see the ways they managed island life. Bardsey had been inhabited until 1925, when the 'King of Enlli', Love Pritchard, took his people to the mainland to live an easier life. At that time there were fewer than 100 living on the island. Soon after that others had moved in and started to farm.

I knew that Bardsey was a good place for watching wild birds. Somewhere I had read of barrowloads of dead birds wheeled away from the base of the lighthouse on Bardsey after a night of migration. Then school lessons in Welsh history had told me of a great monastery where the inspiring number of twenty thousand saints were reputed to be at rest. And from time to time I had seen in the paper that – for instance – its king was ill, or had uttered some profound piece of wit or soothsaying, or was deposed, or had resigned, and that the famous tin crown of Bardsey was upon a younger head.

As an islander myself I was especially eager to find out how far the people of Bardsey were imbued with an 'island complex' such as I have suffered from so fiercely all my life. In their reactions to a confined life should I see the reflections of the many moods, both black and golden, which I had experienced on Skokholm? I was willing to learn from their psychological state how wise or unwise I had been in playing so earnestly at Crusoe. I went to Bardsey too as the ambassador of those young people who – because we on Skokholm seemed so obviously happy – had been questioning me ever since I had started writing about Skokholm in *The Countryman*. They wanted to know if they could get out of their daily ruts in cities, and if they could establish somewhere, collectively, an island autonomy where modern luxuries could be exchanged for the freedom to think and do in the fresh air and to live by home-produced goods. I knew Bardsey supported a community which lived as near this way as any other I had heard of. So I went to see for myself, and I went in the middle of the winter. No-one had studied the bird life at that season, and if one wanted to discover the peculiarities and the moods of the islanders, then these surely might be best observed under the influence of the winter, with its changeable winds and black skies. In the quiet bliss of summer they would be forgetting or minimizing their hardships and their discontents.

The big motor-boat from Bardsey dropped anchor beyond the reach of the breakers in Aberdaron Bay, and five young men, overflowing a dinghy, shot through the surf to greet me with broad grins as I waded out to catch the prow. I was glad of that warm greeting. I had waited a cold November day and a night on this Caernarvon shore, in sight of Snowdon, and had been told that I might easily have to wait a week or two for the island boat. The people of Bardsey have no incentive to fly for shelter to the mainland; for the coast is more naked and inhospitable than the island, where there is a good haven for boats. This fact, I think, makes the islanders the more contented with their home.

Two hours later, when the five young men had sold their exports of butter, chickens, eggs, rabbits, and a pig, and posted the outgoing mail, we all returned with the imports – a carpenter, a full G.P.O. satchel, sacks of flour and maize, groceries – while behind us was the dinghy stacked high with bundles of withies for lobster-pot making.

A race almost as fierce as our Wild Goose of Skokholm leaps between Bardsey and the end of Lleyn, but that day it was too calm at the shift of tide even to prove my seaworthiness to the islanders. For five miles we steered straight for the mountainous lump of the island, the crew laughing and talking in Welsh.

We came in close under the great hill of Bardsey. The sun had fallen down behind it, leaving us to grope in the shadow against the unfriendly cliff. As we coasted along the boat sidled crabwise in the oily ripples of a tideway.

I looked up at the almost sheer hill above us. Only a strayed sheep, a raven and a falcon could be seen along the height. Bardsey has turned its back on the world. To go there is to lose all sight and sound of the mainland – unless you are willing to climb 548 feet to the top of that wild hill to look back at Wales.

Suddenly we swung round the southern shoulder of the cliff, ran down and excitedly captured treasure trove in the form of an empty chest floating on the current; and then we brought up in a low, sandy harbour. There was something very satisfying and grateful in that unexpected transition from high precipice to low fields. Bardsey is like that. There is no half-way scene. A mountain has been crudely cemented to a lowland valley and the whole thrown into the middle of a violent tide-race.

In the gathering darkness the boat was cradled and drawn up on rails out of the sea. We made our way to where lights shone at intervals along the village street, and to the house called Cristin. I had swelled the population of twelve men – including the pastor and three lightkeepers – eight women, ten boys, and five girls to a round three dozen. All spoke English, but most of them haltingly and with a soft Welshness that pleased the ear. Their warm smiles and greetings made me feel I was among a gentle and intelligent people.

About the Bardsey houses there is nothing of the romantic squalor which pervades the small farms of North Wales. Far from it. In Cristin the first thing that greeted me was a wonderful aroma of cooked goose; then I found a neat room with a cheerful coal fire, a brilliant paraffin lamp, a highly selective wireless set, and books – a Welsh Bible, a *Catalogue of Welsh Books,* and volumes of *Punch* and *The Argosy* and Liam O'Flaherty's *Black Soul.* That interior was more or less typical of all the houses on the island.

Early next morning, looking down from the five-hundred-feet hill, I decided that nothing could be agriculturally more enchanting than the two hundred little green fields, most of them less than an acre in extent, which lie between the high street and the sea. The one road does not wander over the fertile lowland of Bardsey, wasting good ground. It climbs straight from the harbour to the foot of the mountain, and there, running over hard rock, becomes a sharp dividing line between the right lowland soil and the barren stony upland. Along it the farmhouses nestle in pairs like mated birds.

I climbed through the furze to the top of the hill and looked out towards the mainland shore and the pyramidal hills of Lleyn as they ride boldly up to the mist-wrapped precipices of Snowdon. From the peak the outlines of a built path guided me more quickly than I had come back to Cristin and a breakfast of home-produced bread-and-butter, bacon and eggs. This path had been built by the late Sir

Spencer Bulkeley Wynn, the owner of Bardsey, so that whenever he took up his residence in the island he could climb the hill in comfort. And no doubt, I thought, he felt the same pleasure as I had felt at the sight of man's neat work in those two hundred little fields far below.

I now began to sound John Evans about why he lived in what most people would think a desolate spot.

'It is as good as any other,' he affirmed, with a pleasant Welsh intonation to his voice. 'I am really very happy. I like quietness and I like the sea. Yes, I am indeed content.'

In a little while, however, I got a more satisfying answer. The fun of being a Crusoe had never occurred to him. As a poor man he had come to the island for no other reason than to make money.

'The rent is very low, less than ten shillings an acre for land twice as fertile and sweet as on the mainland. The buildings are the best in Wales. There are no rates or taxes. And for every pound rent we pay we are entitled to keep one sheep on the mountain. The big motor-boat is maintained by the estate; we only pay a share in its cost of upkeep, at the rate of three and sixpence for every pound of our rent. Yes, I am quite happy. There is good money at the lobstering in the summer. And you are obliged to save your earnings, for there is nowhere to spend them.'

'How long do you intend to live here?'

'I think all of us are saving money because one day we think we shall have enough to go and live in a larger place on the mainland. But even if I had enough I am not sure that I would go. I feel content and free from care here, and he is a dull fellow who knows not the right side of his bread-and-butter.'

'Then why did the last lot of people leave?'

'I suppose they were getting old and did not want to die away from their kin. And no doubt they had stored away a few pounds. Bardsey is a young man's island today. No-one draws the pension here.'

Outside the window we heard the sharp cry of the 'bran goch', as the islanders called the chough. Each morning a pair danced down over the house to feed, crying out as they passed. I was at home, with the sound of the sea and the greeting of this rare bird in my ears as at Skokholm. I went to the window. In the garden below me marigolds, daisies, pinks, chrysanthemums, nasturtiums, and love-in-a-mist were still flowering.

Bardsey windows do not look out upon the dung-heap, as is usual in Welsh farms. They are better planned than that. They look out upon walled-in gardens which slope away below them to the edge of the chessboard of fields, and so to the blue of St George's Channel, with the line of surf on the western shore, and at the far south point the red and white tower of the lighthouse. A man of imagination has built the farms of Bardsey. For the class of small-holding they represent, both the houses and buildings outshine those of many hundred-acre farms on the mainland. It was a happy thought to have paired off the farms so that they might stand shoulder to shoulder to wind and weather. These semi-detached houses, though they have not the charm of age – often the only recommendation of many an otherwise squalid and unimaginative building – have both form and, because they are solidly built to ensure the weather, harmony with their environment. Even the windows reflect the original ideas of their designer. The large sashes are fixed and have twenty-four panes. In addition there is one six-pane sliding sash without cords. It is adjusted with a notched stick, and this is really wisdom in a place of high winds and no carpenters. Each house has on the ground floor from three to five living-rooms, plus scullery and dairy; while upstairs there are three, four, or five bedrooms, according to the acreage of the farm. There are ten farms, and they vary in size between thirteen and thirty acres, not counting the rougher cliff grazings.

John Evans told me that the farmhouses had been built about sixty years ago by the same Sir Spencer who had ordered that path to be cut to the top of the mountain, and the more I studied their arrangement the more I admired the work of a master. Sir Spencer and the mountain were becoming the two dominating features of the island. Each pair of semi-detached houses share a farmyard between them, with ample room for each man to house three cows, a horse, and pigs. And each man shares a cart with his neighbour. Each yard is built four-square to the weather, a miniature fortress, with walls two feet thick at the top, and unpretentiously castellated – as if Sir Spencer wished to emphasize their strength. You enter each yard through a handsome archway. I was told – but I do not know how true it is – that the considerable cost of these buildings was met out of the sum received for the lighthouse site and for the right to collect shipping dues, the landlord desiring to put back into the island money that it made.

In the afternoon I strolled upon the chessboard, watching birds. In these little fields there were white sheep, small and fat, nibbling a sweet turf as green and neat as a billiard-table; small cattle, pure black and very fat, that produce a butter famed well beyond North Wales; stout roan colts and horses of middle breed, some of them swinging up the short furrows before the plough, with clouds of herring-gulls and a stray chough close behind; and grey geese so fat with endless grazing of the clover-filled pasture that they could not even flap themselves over Bardsey's low hedges.

Although it was midwinter, there were still wildflowers in the grass, milkwort, speedwells, spearwort, corn marigolds, and clover, while the southward slant of each bank was alight with furze.

In my passage through the fields I kept stumbling upon little high-banked enclosures, each scarcely larger than a large room, filled with growing willows and watered by the main 'river' – some eighteen inches wide – which meandered hard by. These hidden withy beds delighted me. Contrasted with the bare brown and green fields, they were as striking as a sunlit clearing in a dark wood. And they were always full of birds. In one I surprised two sparrow-hawks plucking a starling, in another a reed-bunting was feeding, in a third I found a water-rail. In the planning of these coverts I saw once more – but I may be wrong – the hand of the imaginative Sir Spencer. The withies are used for making lobster-pots. They were also used formerly for making baskets and creels to hold seaweed and to carry produce to the mainland. Half the wands were cut back to the stools after one year's growth, and half after two years, to provide rods of varying thickness and length. They are badly kept today, yielding perhaps half what they might give with proper hoeing and replanting, and the islanders are obliged to import extra ones to make up their requirements for the fishing season.

In walking down the crisp rows of turnips, swedes, and carrots I flushed redwings, thrushes, larks, and many other birds. At that time of day each farmer is cutting a sackful of tops. The turnips and swedes yield three cuttings in a mild winter. The green tops are mixed with other greens, such as onion spears and cabbage leaves, and with crushed oats and barley. Second-year furze, green and tender, is chopped up with hay and straw in the chaff-cutter, and the whole ration is fed to both cow and horse as a nightcap after the day's grazing. All but two farms have engines to drive their chaff-cutters, corn-grinders, and churns. At one farm the engine runs a dynamo to charge the wireless batteries on the island. The engineless farmers manage well enough with that device of an earlier generation, the horse-table; the man feeds the chaffer, and the wife leads the horse that turns it. Green turnip-tops are cut every day. The furze, involving laborious work with a sharp sickle, is cut three times a week and carried to the machine in a 'burden' twice as large as a man, but on a man's back.

With the oldest landholder, whom I judged to be fifty, I had many a long talk, though we had to struggle between his scanty English and my bad Welsh. In case I should be tempted to take up the one vacant farm he taught me the outlines of his farming methods. He cropped his fields in this rotation: oats after old pasture; roots and potatoes; barley, clover, and rye-grass; clover and hay; pasture. For manure in the old days the islanders used to carry up seaweed from the shore in home-made creels. Later a cart was used, and a road was made along the low line of the western shore so that weed might be picked up at any point. Most of the weed torn up by the Atlantic storms is deposited by a trick of the currents and the twist of the shore in the sandy curve of Porth Solfach, but today little of it is used on account of the heavy labour of lifting the tangled stuff, and it lies there rotting.

My friend complained that men were not what they were. It hurt his economical soul to see good manure wasted. I told him it was not wasted. Untroubled by the terrible stench, were not the crows, choughs, starlings, oyster-catchers, redshanks, turnstones, purple sandpipers, and gulls forever prying and sorting the reeking mass for the rich harvest of the grubs of flies and other larvae with which it was seething? With tons of weed rotting in Port Solfach the place had already become to me as much of an attraction as a sewage farm is to the mainland ornithologist.

The carpenter who had come over with me was employed by sanction of the island Government, which controlled a special fund levied for the purpose. His job was to repair the cattle-boat. He was white-haired and a man of parts who could lead a song and play the instrument common to Welsh homes, the harmonium. And while the gale blew it was pleasanter to be singing or telling a tale than to be rusting one's tools in the wind and rain outside. Hence he would pass one day in hospitality at one house, another day at another, the next at Cristin, and so on. Wherever he went he had a good following to laugh at his tales or to swing into the chorus of an old Welsh song, begun by himself or from the loudspeaker tuned in to the Welsh programme. But even without this incentive, the people of Cristin were for ever singing, as is the habit of Welsh folk, and since I did not know the words I was as agreeably mystified and charmed as if they had been singing Russian folk-songs. They were careful to practise their tonic sol-fa each evening, so that the youngest might learn this serious business properly, and do himself credit, first at chapel and last, perhaps, at the Eisteddfod.

But to hear the whole island in song you must go to evening chapel, which is no hardship, for there is no collection. The little children stand up beneath the pulpit and say your prayers very prettily for you, and it has to be over and done with quickly because the youngest must be in bed early. If it is a very violent and disagreeable day you need not go at all, for the chapel is at the far north end of the island, or if you do you will be the only one who is not listening in to a Welsh service at home.

6

Summer on Skokholm

(around 1933)

We have two larks singing on the island. They begin long before sunrise, but not before the oyster-catchers are awake and trilling their loud reveille: 'Awake! Awake! Wake, wake, wake . . .'

From midnight until 2 a.m. the shearwaters utter their unearthly screams, quite drowning the soft crooning notes which come from the storm-petrels nesting in the hedges and walls. Impossible to describe the shearwaters' call – beyond hinting that it suggests a catcall and a cockcrow uttered simultaneously and cut off with a sharp knife before the finish. At 2.30 a.m. the wheatears exchange a few sharp notes. Then Jonathan, our Rhode Islander, gives out his fine challenge, though there is no other cock to answer him. Soon the sea-pies wake up from their uneasy sleep and rouse our world with their clamour. The gulls begin complaining and the larks go up to heaven.

When from the low window we see the sun shining on a placid sea, barely rippled by the headstrong tide, when all the far headlands are bathed in the strong light, we too are invigorated. It may be that there is not a breath of wind to rustle the purple sea-spurrey growing on the lintel. The loveliness of the world enchants us we grow excited. Or it may be that the fine weather tempted us to sleep in the heather. How eagerly we rush down for the morning dive in the harbour How impatient are the goats to be milked and freed from their night stall!

We sing as we lay breakfast outdoors. We hasten to wash up afterwards and to finish all the tiresome household duties. Then comes the consideration of the day's work.

The programme is soon laid out. I am to cut peat in the morning while Doris does some necessary housework, including the making of one of her incomparable rabbit pies. We are to fish in the afternoon to replenish a depleted larder.

The coal from the wreck of the *Alice Williams* having dwindled to the last few tons, we save these for special baking days and for very cold weather. With care, this remnant should see us beyond another winter. The island 'peat', which is really little better than consolidated layers of turf, burns well, if quickly, with a deep-hearted glow, and with a log of driftwood to make a bright flame is splendid in the capacious grate of the living-room. Even when we are out of coal, Doris proposes to cook with peat in the old-fashioned way. Of course there is plenty of driftwood, and, as usual in summer, we have accumulated a great pile, ready for the winter fires.

Spade on shoulder I go out to dig my turves on the island bog, and spread them out to dry. They have then to be stacked to dry, and are finally taken home, to go under cover, with Punch [*the pony*] in the light cart assisting.

At noon it was cooler, a breeze coming out of the west. I was very hungry, and dined greedily off rabbit pie, new peas and potatoes, followed by stewed rhubarb and junket, everything home-produced, like the goat's milk we had with our morning porridge. Then I weeded in the garden for an hour, and afterwards went out to sea with Doris to haul two dozen lobster-pots. Fairly good result: one crayfish, two small lobsters and five crabs. We also had a giant conger eel in one pot, but could do nothing with it, so saved it to give to the lightkeepers. Thousands of puffins, guillemots and razorbills were diving for sprats in the harbour, while the kittiwake gulls snatched those feeding on the surface. Whence came these myriads of sprats at such an opportune time to feed all the young broods in July and August?

And so to tea, strawberries and cream, brown bread and lemon curd, and cake. The strawberries we manage to grow in a sheltered corner of the garden are few but fine; the curd Doris makes from fresh gulls' eggs in season.

The goats and the sheep have often an inconvenient habit of moving along the coast all day as they browse and ending up at the far end for the night, a mile from the house. We agreed to round them all up tonight, but that on our way we would put numbered rings on the legs of one hundred razorbills. Razorbills are likely to be profitable. A number ringed as nestlings in July in Scotland were recovered on the Scandinavian coast in November – a curious migration.

The west wind had increased to nearly a gale as we walked over to Mad Bay, where our greatest colonies of razorbills hide their eggs and downy young. Down among the boulders and talus of the bay we searched. Beneath the red rocks the handsome black and white adults stood guard over their solitary youngster. The oldsters growl alarmingly at you, while the babies squeak in a high, thin pipe. It is not easy to corner the old birds; they make a dash for safety if they see their chance. Even when caught they bite severely – as our wrists soon testified – with their sharp razor bills. We managed, nevertheless, to ring at least a dozen adults.

'Grr . . . rr!'

'Quick, I've got one! A ring, please!'

A ring is quickly clipped on one leg, its number noted, and the bird released. The young ones were easy to ring, and we went along at a fine pace, for they were plentiful under every piece of broken cliff.

The tide and wind had been steadily rising. The smooth water of a calm summer day was now transformed into a series of giant swells, which, rank after rank, flung themselves on the work red cliffs and into the deep caves, throwing the spray ever higher and higher. The setting sun shone brightly and threw a bow into every tall column of spray. The lowermost razorbills were anxious about their young ones; those with eggs were safe; but the heavy spray ran back in streams over the cliff, and many a baby we found sitting in a pool, cold and numb.

The adult razorbills sitting on the tops of the lower rocks made the prettiest scene when they flew high up in the air all together each time a high wave threatened them, mingling delightfully with the spray and the rainbows against the background of red cliff, with its green thrift and yellow lichen.

There was so much to find and see that evening that the sun set long before we were ready for it. We came on a valuable piece of timber wedged in the rocks, to say nothing of firewood. We found hundreds of other birds, nests, eggs and young. We trembled when we came across the young gulls who were grown enough to be able to walk confidently to the edge, ready, heedless of their lives, to take the plunge into the raging sea if we approached a foot too near. A tiny storm-petrel was brooding its egg in an unexpected position, in the centre of a flat stretch of wind-blown sand beneath high boulders. A young shearwater was cunningly placed in a slit in a rock. Here and there were crowded bunches of guillemots, their once bright green eggs thickly bedaubed with the muck of their colony. A few had hatched, however, just to prove that the coating of filth made no difference to successful incubation.

That evening we were lucky enough to see a seal feeding.

In a narrow creek out of the wind, where the backwash from the waves nevertheless made angry white water, a huge dark seal – it must have been an old bull – had just caught a giant brown skate, and was doing battle with it. The fish was fully three-fourths the length of the seal, if the long tail be included, and a good deal wider. The seal had gripped the skate in the vital spot in the centre of its white under-side, and although the fish now lashed the seal furiously with its tail, and anon struck blows with its wide 'wings', the issue was scarcely in doubt. Placing its two paws tightly around the skate, and gripping it with extended claws, the seal tore the mouthful he already possessed completely out of the fish and, tossing up his head, swallowed it with a few gulps. Again and again he tore and swallowed.

The sun had long set when we actually used our last ring and came to the end of the more accessible colonies in Mad Bay. It was long past milking time, but we had spent a happy evening, and as we drove home the goats we felt tired.

'Tomorrow will do', we agreed, looking at the sheep comfortably chewing the cud in a sheltered bay, and we did not disturb them that night. In the sky the new moon was very low. Doris bowed three times. She always does.

While I was milking I heard the night birds coming in. When the moon had set, the first shearwaters came screaming home. They the breeding cry – I suppose really the love-song – of our well-loved storm-petrels. It is not often they are heard on the wing, and here was one flying round and round about the goat-house. I put down my pail and ran to fetch Doris. Together we watched the little birds flying, calling, and chasing each other in their excitement. Their tiny forms loomed but faintly in the dark, but we saw them well when they brushed past our faces, forgetful or heedless of our nearness.

7

Experiments on Skokholm
(1934)

I look back on the latest records of the Island birds and beasts. We love to study and experiment with these subjects of ours. But I find the birds have been very whimsical this year. More than half of my prepared nesting sites have been deserted.

I took a pane out of the wheelhouse window to give the swallows free entry; but they built their nest in a little wooden hut in which we store the pony's hay. I made a number of holes in the garden walls and placed heaps of stones with dug-outs beneath them for the storm-petrels; they laid instead beneath a disused door, in a butter-box, and under a peat-hag. I scythed the bracken about the wall to discourage the whitethroats, which had ousted the sedge-warblers, but the meadow-pipits came instead, and the whitethroats only moved farther on.

Because I burnt all the old heather for the sake of the sea-pies, the wheatears and the sheep, the stonechats nested away on the mainland, but they were good enough to bring back a fledged brood to feed in the garden.

The choughs hung about so late that I felt sure of a nest by June, yet they vanished, and in their place a pair of shags nested in the same ravine in Mad Bay. Then a white owl [barn owl] disappeared too, leaving the island to a silent, evil little owl, whose four eggs were laid upon ninety-eight quill feathers of the storm-petrel (its favourite food here), in a hole under a slab of rock facing the wild tides at the Head.

The ravens reared four, but all through the year the buzzards did naught but line their nest with flowers, and sit about ornamentally, if sluggishly, on the higher rocks. I think the female, a huge hoary bird, has grown too old to lay eggs. They lived exclusively on rabbits until the shearwater exodus began.

Year after year the same pairs of shearwaters return to this colony. The numbered leg-rings they wear grow thinner each year through contact with salt air and water, and are soon defaced. To be on the safe side we now substitute new rings each year. The same pairs keep fairly regularly to the same burrows. AE 688 (or Caroline), our most precious bird, must now be at least eleven years old.

Experiments with puffins, as well as with other sea-birds, are being carried out on the same lines, and meanwhile we have worked out part of the life-history of the young puffin in its first year. Nothing was known of how the young puffin reached the sea. We can now dispel the belief that the parents carry it down. On the contrary, the old puffins, like the shearwaters, suddenly desert the portly fledgling, having overfed him so long, and go off to sea to moult their faded and worn plumage. The young one lives for several days, camel-like, off its own fat. Its high cheeping hunger-call, unanswered, gradually ceases. It remains sitting near the mouth of the burrow, too timid to venture abroad. But at last, after four or five days, the forces it has so long resisted drive it forth from the burrow and into the sea.

Despite the fact that when adults the species is entirely diurnal on land, the young one (and this must be noted as a sign of inherited wisdom) walks to the sea only by night. Nothing is more enchanting than to go out of doors on July and August nights and wander along the cliffs in search of young puffins on the march. Lacking the brilliance of the parents, dark-beaked and footed, they have a sober, dignified air as they leisurely, uprightly, goose-step in the glare of our torch. Coming to a downward slope they will suddenly take wing, not always reaching the sea at the first attempt. We find them in the mornings imprisoned in the garden or in the folds, bewildered after a series of bad take-offs. We take them to the sea, and mark how, on touching the water, they dive and dive, often and long. Only in this manner, by leading a life-half-submarine at sea, and wholly nocturnal on land, until it can learn to fly strongly, does the young puffin defeat the gulls, which would otherwise exterminate it.

This desertion by the parents explained one thing which had puzzled me on the day in August six years ago that I made my second crossing to the island. It explained why I saw the fledgling puffins swimming apart from the groups of adults, never following their parents, as were the young razorbills and guillemots.

Thus you will see that my one-time dreams have come true, for my wife and I dwell on an island, far from the turmoil of a city, and accessible only to the chosen few. If we have few of the modern amenities of civilization, we have in full measure the glory of the sea and the winds and the sky. We have a rich show of sea-loving flowers. We have seals and sheep and goats. We have all the birds we could wish for, and welcome every one; in the summer there are over thirty thousand on our island, of which two-thirds comprise puffins and shearwaters. In variety, so far, well over a hundred different species are recorded, and there is a peculiar delight in welcoming new species in such a well-defined area as an island.

8

Heligoland
(1936)

Ronald Lockley visited other islands (including Ramsey, The Blaskets (off Ireland), Heligoland (off Denmark) and Fair Isle (to the north of Scotland)), and wrote about them in I Know an Island. *The book contains an important comparative record of island lives in the 1930s.*

There were visitors to the observatory on Skomer one year, and one of them invited Ronald to go and see his bird observatory on the island of Heligoland, in the North Sea, roughly north-north-west of Bremerhaven. The island is now a popular holiday resort, but was a disturbing place to be in October 1936, with the Nazis in power. Although Ronald had visited to see the bird observatory, he couldn't help but notice the atmosphere.

Skokholm was twice the size of Heligoland, but almost uninhabited, and Ronald found the life there quite a contrast to his own Dream Island.

Since the coast of Germany is flat and dykebound, the tall red cliffs of Heligoland rising in the Bight twenty-eight miles from the land are considered to be both unique and wonderful by Germans. Add to this attraction a small sand-dune rising out of the sea a mile to the east – just what one wants for bathing and a little harmless Crusoeing – the red roofs of Lower Heligoland below the red cliffs, the buffs and greens of the house walls of Upper Town above these cliffs, the whole surmounted by a tall church spire and a still taller lighthouse, and we have the ingredients of one of those miraculous-looking islets pictured in fairy-tale books.

I took the surprisingly grand *Hamburg-Amerika* day ship and crossed in two and a half hours. On the way over an old Heligolander with whom I made acquaintance prepared me for the surprise of finding an island half as small as Skokholm supporting a population of three thousand. He had never lost British citizenship – that right had been guaranteed him when England exchanged Heligoland for Zanzibar.

On August 9 1890, Henry Hedger, English coastguard, lowered the Union Jack from the Governor's flagstaff at Heligoland, as the island was then called by English people – probably from the 'Hilligelunn' of the native dialect, a curious hybrid of English and Scandinavian, which is now said to be dying out under the influence of 'pure' Nazi German. At the same moment and for the same reason the German flag was lowered on Zanzibar Island, East Africa.

This was a sad hour for the two thousand people of Heligoland who had so long enjoyed an easy freedom under British protection – a freedom much valued by a race faithful to its traditions and quaint language. The Heligolanders had paid no taxes, and no man had been obliged to serve the Queen for any year of his young life. My friend, however, with several others, had joined her Majesty's Navy, the island being noted for its export of daring pilots and sailors at that time. As a port Heligoland was the second free harbour in Europe (Copenhagen is the first). Because of its unique cliffs, remoteness, and charm it attracted a well-to-do class, fed at little cost from the untaxed provisions discharged upon its wharf. It was well known as a cheap victualling place for ships in the North Sea.

But if life was easy and profitable to the inhabitants under an English governor it was also unenterprising. The men still fished, used old methods of their forefathers, hunting for haddock and cod with a fleet of sloops. About a hundred fishermen manned some thirty-two sloops, which often made courageously long voyages along the coast following the North Star and their luck.

The harbour was inadequate and dangerous. Often during gales the small lobstering boats had to be dragged up among the houses on the strand, while sloops had to ride out at moorings that were frequently carried away. Fishermen lived heroically, using their boats as lifeboats, manoeuvring them through the shoals that beset the island to some schooner or brig driven aground. The streets of the town were badly paved and ill-lighted, and there was no drainage. Water was a problem – there is no natural spring on the island.

England might have made of Heligoland a formidable naval-supply and mine-laying base from which, my friend said, in wartime, aided by the local knowledge of Heligoland pilots, she could have hemmed in the whole of the German fleet. But England did nothing. Queen Victoria added a bell-tower to the church, and the garrison manned a gun or two for the same of appearances. The people were interfered with not at all.

Then came the Heligoland-Zanzibar change-over. A clause in the Anglo-German agreement exempted all men born under English rule from service in the German army or navy. The Germans instantly began fortifications on the grand scale. The harbour and communications were improved, artillery barracks built, and it was said that there was enough money, between the bustle of building and the summer visitors, to pave the streets with gold. Every road and path was bricked or tiled over, including a promenade along the whole of the top of the cliffs (this had another purpose too – to prevent rain washing away the edges of the very soft rock). In the old days all goods and building materials were humped on the fishermen's backs up the hundred and eighty steps of the cliff stairs. The Germans built a two-way lift, and drove a tunnel through the heart of the cliff to connect the upper and lower towns. The island was rapidly modernized, but fortunately the good taste of the Germans ensured a happy blending of the new with the old. Guns are the only conspicuous incongruities today.

On August 1, 1914, a large steamer anchored off the island. It had come to evacuate the two thousand inhabitants. They were given an hour to pack no more than could be carried in the hand. The heavy gear, bedding, and furniture must be left until the War was won in a few weeks' time. All men who had once been in the British services were arrested without an opportunity even to clap a hat on their heads – a precaution illustrating German thoroughness, for Britain had not yet declared war upon Germany. But, although these men could not be required to join the German army or navy, they knew too much of the coast and the fortifications to be allowed the smallest chance of escaping abroad. It was hard for them, mostly veterans on pension, to be herded into internment camps, for of the aged, people, men and women, imprisoned or otherwise, few were to survive to see their beloved island again. This was the dark moment when no Heligolander remained to lift and salute the island tricolour. Thus was broken a spell of occupation said to have begun before the time of Christ.

During the whole of the Great War the guns on Heligoland were never called upon to speak to an enemy. The battle of Jutland was out of their reach. My friend had heard it said that the garrison was so bored with their island existence that they turned to the cellars of the absent natives for consolation, and on these occasions the island might have been taken by a handful of the enemy. But gossip of this sort is easier to hear than to believe.

On December 5, 1918, a dismal winter day, a steamer left Hamburg with the sadly reduced 1914 population of Heligoland. There were tears and cries of joy from the weary and hysterical people as the deep red cliffs of their island home showed up: 'Ach, Helgoland! Unser Heim! Schön Helgoland!'

'Ah, beautiful Heligoland!' said my friend. 'But you can well imagine that wild storms in four years had shaken many of the old-fashioned red-tiled roofs. The little homes were in a terrible condition. Fungi and salt were encrusted upon the inner walls. The wallpaper hung in shreds. The floors were green and rotten. The gardens were choked with weeds, the white palings were blown down, the paving tiles were lifted up by grass.'

Those who had the heart to claim compensation for lost business and damaged property were reminded that even if they were paid a billion marks they could scarcely buy a loaf of bread with it, so low had the mark fallen. Penniless and hungry, the islanders set to work to put their homes in order, to paint and distemper, the polish the silver and brass name-plates and door-handles which are the pride of every cottager in Heligoland, to prop up fences and to dig gardens.

Then work came unexpectedly. Under the supervision of English officers the fortifications and the submarine base were to be destroyed completely. So well had these been built, however, that it took three years to reduce the moles, plug the tunnels, and blow up the machinery.

Twelve years after the destruction of the fortifications the Germans began building them on an even more gigantic scale. The dynamiting during the demolition was bad enough, but when the great new guns speak it is believed that every window will be shattered, and the unstable cliffs slide down to the sea. Still, for the present rebuilding means work, and probably there are over three thousand people crowded today upon the forty acres of the housing quarter, and there are four hundred children attending school in the morning.

Two thousand passengers can be accommodated on the twice-weekly winter steamer, which brings this load every fine day in the summer. Other ships may call and discharge a few more thousand sightseers, until as many as nine thousand have thronged the narrow streets. There have been critical hours at the time of embarking on summer days, said my friend, when no one could move one way or the other and the officials were at their wits' end! Walking room is limited to the streets and the promenade around the island. The rest is a prohibited area – fortress and docks.

Ronald spent some days at the Fanggarten, or bird-catching garden. He walked there on the first morning with Dr Rudolf Drost, the German ornithologist who ran the bird observatory on the island. The observatory had been made famous by Heinrich Gätke.

On our walk through the town we had seen birds everywhere, perching on every house and fence and in every bush and plant in the tiny gardens. Song-thrushes and robins predominated. We passed one woman scrubbing the roadway – all citizens must keep the road outside their houses spotless, for dirt is forbidden and litter must be jettisoned through a chute into the sea. There were two robins perching, exhausted, upon the woman's head.

My lodgings are comfortable. Electricity brightens the little houses here. Water has to be imported if the amount collected in underground tanks from the wooden eaves-gutters runs low. Heligoland rainwater is said to be of a very good flavour because of the earthenware tiles and the wooden gutters, but I was also told that it often tastes gamy; this is due to the great number of small birds that drop exhausted down the pipes leading to the tanks on a night of heavy migration.

Sunday October 25: Not many people go to church. There is a dance-hall. At the cinema, where films are changed weekly, saw today a very poor show: a dull, stale newsreel, and two or three films frankly propagating the Nazi cause – road-making scenes, marching, counter-marching, goose-stepping, and fierce speeches. Yet nearly four hundred people, or about an eighth of the population, filled the building, so that most of the folk must see the films in a seven-day week.

Yesterday there had been a demonstration by some political organization – I did not know what – at which all young men had to attend. And almost every day a new 'thought' appears on the notice-boards on the staircase joining Upper and Lower Towns. I notice that 'Bolshevismus' and 'Return our Colonies' seem to be the two most burning themes. All this, and the 'Fly your Swastika' and other patriotic law and etiquette, combined with the swarms of people in the streets, is suggestive of the law, order, and communism of the ant-heap – warriors and workers complete.

October 27: A great gale from the west, the waves leaping in clouds over the naval base and sweeping into the streets of Lower Town. No steamer could come. The tug standing by in the roads disappeared. Nearly half little Dune Islet was swept away, many people with telescopes watching the buildings upon it crumble and slide into the sea. Finally came the news that the lightship *Elbe 3*, between Heligoland and Hamburg, had capsized and sunk with all hands. The whole shallow sea was perfectly white, as I have never seen the deep water of the Atlantic in its worst mood. Yet when I struggled back to my lodgings in Upper Town I found them quite sheltered in the lee of many other houses, and the few roses still out in my host's garden were scarcely stirring in the wind.

October 28: Drost and I parted over Gätke's grave in the churchyard in the heart of Upper Town, and I went down the stairs to an impatient steamer blowing for passengers and anxious to get back out of the wild weather.

Two things which I saw as the steamer moved off remained vivid in my mind's eye for long after. The first was the great red cliffs with their ledges on which in summer the guillemots breed. I thought of Gätke's nice description of these birds:

> Amid the exchanges of endless obeisances and incessant altercations they carry on an animated conversation in which every one of them seems to be talking, and none listening.

The other impression was of the yellow sands of the Dune Islet, now much eroded.

All Heligoland, all Germany, was in mourning today. We dipped the swastika as we steamed slowly past the site of the lost *Elbe 3*. A new ship, with the same label freshly painted on her hull, was already being anchored in position, while close by the steam tender was dragging the shallow water for her predecessor.

9

Life on Skokholm

(about 1937)

In this extract Ronald observes his life on Skokholm. He had been there for ten years by that time, Doris for slightly less.

We have, I dare say, been selfish in never regarding ourselves as examples for the rest of the world to follow. We have taken island life much as we have found it. Were we to leave Skokholm now the storms would quickly reduce the buildings to their former ruinous state, and in a few years the island would be as wild and as unkempt as it was when I arrived in 1927. For we have had no capital on which we might lotus-eat, with which we might build castles and walled gardens. We have done everything with our hands, and our efforts, after all, have been puny and ephemeral enough. I have no doubt but that the casual visitor today thinks that the island and the buildings on it are in a sorry state. But he should have seen Skokholm when we found it.

As long as the coal from the *Alice Williams* lasted winter gales could be laughed at. While the little island house shuddered in the cool Atlantic hurricanes all was aglow within doors, where our red-tiled hearth supported bonfires of the fierce gas coal with a log of driftwood on top sporting blue salt-flame. But after five years the supply suddenly gave out, and we had to turn to the turf or peat and driftwood only. We were more careful then; we had to nurse our wood store. At times we were short, for at first I under-estimated the amount of turf we should need. But rather than import coal – a filthy business for man and boat – we burned clumps of old heather and thrift until we had dried out a fresh supply of turf.

Those were the best years, those summers and winters of shepherding on the island. With Ann yet too young for school the summers were idylls of fishing, swimming, sailing, and basking, when the body acquired a tan which lasted throughout the winter. We lived on garden produce, fish, rabbits, goats; milk, kids, sheep and honey. And we shared the daily work of house-cleaning, washing our simple clothes and utensils, gardening, collecting gulls' eggs and driftwood, digging peat, fishing, watching birds, and listing flowers.

Winters I remember as two intermingled seasons: first there were the days of cold, clear, vivid calm synchronized with the sound of migrating birds – huge flocks of lapwing, geese, and golden plover rushing past by night and day; and secondly there were the days of roaring wind that turned the cheeks red and made movement out of doors an exhilarating, breathless struggle, when the house was a glorious sanctuary of warmth.

Wind always meant work in collecting driftwood, which it piled up on the windward shores of the island. We cut paths to every little bay, zigzagging down the campion-hung cliffs. You could run headlong down these paths, so strongly did the wind blow up them and support you. On the return your bulging sack of jetsam acted as a sail to bring you to the top again. Some logs needed block and tackle. The cross-cut was kept well sharpened for the daily cutting-up in such weather. I dare say, altogether, wood for the fires took up nearly two hours' work each winter's day once the coal was exhausted. And with house-work and shepherding the day slipped past. At dusk the goats were milked in their stalls. At nine in the evening we were nodding for sleep before a dying fire, my wife making or mending the family garments, myself with the day-book – recording flowers, birds, and beasts seen – in my lap.

How far out of touch we were with the normal life of the mainland, country and town, I realised acutely when – hesitatingly, be it said – I answered an invitation to broadcast. I went to London. It was a shock to be among the jaded-looking, pale faces of the men and women, to cram and crush in stuffy tubes and buses, to breathe the fumes of burned oil with which the streets stink, to feel dizzy with the roar of the traffic. The feeble flicker of herd excitement in me soon vanished, succeeded by a feeling of despair that the control of nation and wealth should be centred in and dependent on these people. It seemed to me that they were living hopeless, meaningless lives – the unrest and discontent which I seemed to read in their faces I took to be due to an unnatural craving for money, for the false and intangible security of monetary wealth. There was none of the peace and natural well-being which you may find in the rugged face of the poor but healthy countryman. I hurried back to breathe the island air, weary of auditions, revising proofs, and seeing people who tried to entertain, answer the telephone, and dictate all at once.

London seemed to have dug its tentacles deep beyond even the Home Counties. I did not breathe happily until the Welsh mountains loomed up. It was comforting to remember the shepherds who, strong in body and mind, held those mountains in content and peace as we held our island. My despairing wish was that all men should live in peace and plenty in the country, forswearing evil struggle and diabolical invention.

One day on the mainland Ann said that the grass hurt her eyes. That brought suddenly home to us her lack of experience of the mainland. I had noticed in other springtimes the queer faint little pain that the sight of lane grass, lush and deep green, had brought to eyes long attuned to the blues of sea and sky, the red of the island rocks, and the insipid green of rabbit-grazed turf. Only seafarers will appreciate the entirely physical sensation.

Thereafter we took Ann on expeditions into the hinterland of Pembrokeshire. So long had we left these scenes that we found ourselves deep in a youthful wonder at sight of new-budding trees. We recaptured unexpectedly those first raptures of young days exploring in the early summer woods and fields, remembering with a vivid pleasure half-forgotten flowers birds, animals, butterflies. It was all in deep contrast with the naked, clear beauty of the island those still, heavy-hanging shadowed trees, fields deep in clover and grain; the farm animals lacking the alertness of island creatures.

In September 1934, Ronald and Doris decided to sell their sheep and farming gear, and ferried everything to the mainland to hold a sale. They were planning to concentrate on bird-study. Ronald had written several articles for the press on the subject, which had 'already paid better than a year's labour with the sheep'. *They kept the goats and the pony, and some Soay sheep.*

Ann had now to go to school. The goats and pony we could leave in the care of the lighthouse keepers. Winters were therefore free to us. But the lure of islands was strong. If we could not visit others we stole off for a holiday on our own island, drawn by a fine spell following the autumn gales. From our winter house [*the lodge at Martinshaven*] on the mainland opposite the island we were in sight and sound of the portents of a good day for crossing to Skokholm – fine weather and quiet sea.

So it has come to this – that we winter on the coast opposite the island. Like the guillemots, we pay it day-visits in midwinter; like the puffins, we return to live on it at the end of March; and, like the storm-petrels, we temporarily abandon it in October.

Single-handed my wife and I could never have carried on properly the rapidly-growing ornithological work; there was so much outdoor observation to be done and so many things to be recorded afterwards. So that we have always been glad to welcome those who have offered to help, who have invaded our summer fastness in the spirit of scientific investigation. But the procession of these 'students' has had to be organised, and as a result Skokholm has now the tag 'Bird Observatory' experimentally attached to it. Observers come prepared to share in all the types of work which a Crusoe existence demands, including painting, repairing, and cleaning their quarters, fetching and carrying and washing up. We have rebuilt some of the old buildings to accommodate this new 'staff'.

But the island does not overflow with these enthusiasts. Even at the best times for bird-watching we can take no more than ten observers – this figure is considered the limit if interference with nesting birds is to be avoided. And luckily the island is too inaccessible for the average day-visitor, so that trippers do not trouble us at all.

At the end of March when we return to the island there is much to do. We have to repair the havoc done to the bird-ringing traps by the winter gales. The house itself must be distempered inside and whitewashed outside. The garden needs to be dug and planted. The goats, which have run wild all the winter and have kidded earlier in the month, have to be brought into their night stall – a movable shelter which, placed on a fresh piece of grass each night, keeps these animals as sweet and clean as a new apple. The best-looking kids (we are gradually building up a pure white herd) will be kept for stock; the rest will be killed for eating at six weeks.

The chapter continues with long descriptions of the Skokholm Bird Observatory's early work on bird behaviour and migration. Studies were being undertaken on the migratory habits of meadow-pipits, wheatears and kestrels, and on the lives and gustatory preferences of little owls. Gannets ringed four or five years before returned to Grassholm, proving what had hitherto been conjecture – that gannets return to the place of their birth. Manx shearwaters ringed on Skokholm were taken to various places (ranging from Manchester to Venice!) to see if they would return to the island; they did. Ronald recorded:

. . . some curious recoveries of birds ringed by us, such as the gannet that flew on board *HMS Foxhound* when the ship was patrolling the North Spanish coast, the great black-backed gull that was hooked on a fishing-line at Lundy Island, the white-throat that was found drowned in the water-butt at Cheddar, and another that was run over by a car in the Isle of Man; the meadow-pipit shot in South Spain, the razorbill in the Gulf of Genoa, and the shearwater that landed in a colliery-working in the Rhondda Valley. We are now ringing some four to six thousand birds a year on Skokholm. Our recoveries are about 5 per cent.

On some cloudy days of cool westerly wind when it is swept clean of migrants and even the native birds seem well hidden I am moved by the inescapable sense of loneliness and desolation which most of us experience on treeless, windswept islands. It is hard for me to imagine living in a birdless world – the beautiful forms and flight of wild birds always send a pulse of delight through me, even in the most weary moment.

10

Letters from Skokholm

(1947)

From 10 September 1939 to 24 September 1940 – the day the family finally left Skokholm – Ronald Lockley wrote letters to his brother-in-law. John Buxton was familiar with the island, having wardened it for a while earlier that year while Ronald was visiting some Atlantic islands. In 1939, with the onset of war, the Lockleys decided to buy another flock of sheep and farm the island rather more determinedly.

On 10 May 1940, John was captured by the Germans in Norway, and Ronald continued to write to him in the prisoner-of-war camp. At the time, some of these letters had to be carefully checked for place-names; when they were published in 1947, Ronald went through them and replaced the names.

The chapters are dedicated to detailed studies of particular birds and some animals. At the end of the book are Appendices of birds and flowers, with a full census of pairs of breeding birds over thirteen years.

Ronald also shared with John the details of living on Skokholm. Just after the start of the War – 26 September 1939 – their weekly shopping trip to the mainland was described thus:

Our 'outside' problems are principally concentrated into the one day in the week or fortnight in which we make an expedition to the mainland shopping centre at Haverfordwest. Our simple wants have been listed on the island all the week and are then gathered in one furious round of the shops before we hasten to return to the boat. Even as we buy our groceries and goods and hear the shopkeepers' small talk we have one ear cocked for the sound of the wind in the eaves of the town buildings or the tree tops, and an eye for the speed and direction of the clouds overhead. We are more anxious about the return passage to Skokholm than the retail purchases over the counter; and I often find myself, tired of the shop assistant's delay in packing our stores, back in the street for a moment, gazing at the sky. As I do this, sometimes there gathers about me a crowd of idle people who stare up at nothing, and continue to do so long after I have returned indoors, I smiling, they asking each other what is in the sky, or is it an enemy plane?

This tyranny of our appointment with the mainland is a salutary one, for it convinces us that, as long as we have good health and sound limbs and can move actively in our boat, our island is the best place for us. And that until the stiffening of our joints brings a warning of age and the inability to handle engine and oar we are justified in continuing to enjoy Skokholm.

Our mainland visits, then, act as punctuation marks in a life where time becomes almost illimitable, or at least is of less account than season and weather. We often forget which day of the week it is, or we may have to calculate the date by computation, or get it from the radio news, which, however, we are apt to forget to switch on. It is not that we take no interest in the news of the outside world, especially now that war has made news so stirring; it is simply that our normal island duties, whose proper execution is essential to our well-being, absorb our day almost completely.

Those duties are concerned with the economical use of the natural resources of the island, so as to make us, as far as possible, self-supporting. Our day vanishes in the occupations of shepherding, milking goats, catching rabbits and fish, collecting gulls' eggs and driftwood, cultivating two gardens, and digging, drying, carting, and storing peat.

There were a hundred Clun Forest sheep to look after, too, with, in due season, lambing, shearing, dipping, and transporting wool and the lambs to market on the mainland. The family kept a number of goats, Swiss crossed with Welsh. They kept hens, but also collected about two thousand gulls' eggs each spring and preserved them in barrels for cooking. Rabbits made a tasty casserole. They killed a sheep every few months, sharing it with the light-house keepers, and salted the remainder. Cheese could be made from the goats' milk.

The Lockley family were joined on Skokholm in about 1936 by 'the Baron'. He was a Pembrokeshire man who had fought in the Boer War, and spent some time in Canada, before returning to live with his brother in Lawrenny, Pembrokeshire. He was at a loose end, so Ronald and Doris invited him to live on Skokholm with them as a handyman. His real name was George Henry Owen Harries, but his habit of telling highly-coloured stories, based on his own experiences, led Ronald to nickname him the Baron (after Baron Munchausen) and the name stuck. He was a part of the family until the late 1940s. Ronald wrote a book about him, A Pot of Smoke, *published in 1940.*

Of other meat we occasionally eat a woodcock or curlew caught in the bird-traps, and have tried other large birds, such as oyster-catcher, puffin, shearwater, gannet and gull, but only as a novel experiment, rarely repeated. For we are too fond of birds generally to want to kill them even for food, and besides we have a plentiful supply of protein foods in milk, butter, cheese, eggs, rabbits, and fish.

With their lines, Ronald and the Baron caught pollack, mackerel, wrasse, whiting and conger eels, and their pots caught lobsters, crabs, and sometimes crayfish. Doris grew fruit and vegetables in the two gardens – as an insurance, at the first threat of war in 1938, they had started another garden for growing maincrop potatoes. For the fire they collected driftwood and cut peat from the island. They were as self-sufficient as they could be, and determined to stay on Skokholm while the war raged elsewhere in the world.

One of Ronald's tasks was to put identification rings on birds' legs, and then to communicate all his later findings to the Natural History Museum in London. With the help of visiting ornithologists, he set up humane methods of trapping birds, so that he could ring them, measure and weigh them, check their general condition, sex, etc, and then release them.

The ravens that inhabited Skokholm were a constant source of interest to Ronald and his family.

The island is not large enough to contain more than one pair; and I have observed that, except in the autumn, no other raven is tolerated by the residents on Skokholm. Many a day in early spring, or on fine still days in December and January, I have heard them fill the blue sky with angry croakings. On these occasions I have watched our ravens attack other ravens, which, exploring or merely passing by, ventured over the island. These barking cries are very different from the softer, slower, deep, varied, rumbling notes which are used in conversation by the mated pair at the nest, when feeding, and when performing those curious and exciting aerial dances which are indulged in chiefly in early spring. These consist of rolling over sideways in flight, and gliding or flying very short distances upside-down; and often suddenly swooping downwards vertically with closed wings. On the ground the courting raven performs quite a series of bobbings and bowings and caresses to secure the response of his mate.

Our ravens favoured the steep cliffs of Mad Bay as a nesting site. From 1928 to 1939 they only nested twice on the south side of the island. For the rest of the time they had two sites, both close together, one on the north and one on the south face of the same projection in Mad Bay. They changed from one site to the other every other year. It may be that the old nest became rather verminous after two years' occupation and needed a rest for the wind and the weather to spring-clean it. It was a solidly built affair with a foundation of sticks, especially heather twigs, lined with a first lining of mud, grass, and moss, and completed with the hair of our ponies and the wool of our sheep. A very compact and spacious cradle for the three to six blue-green eggs, spotted and blotched with brown, which were laid in February. When incubating, the hen seemed to sit deep in the nest, like a child in a bed too wide for it. But when after three weeks' incubation the eggs were hatched, the nest was quickly filled by the rapidly growing youngsters, and in a very short time they overflowed on to the ledges of the cliff. As they got their glossy feathers they began to push each other out of the nest. There was no longer room for the mother to brood them and the parents had to sleep away from the nest when the chicks were three to four weeks old. A fortnight later, by the end of April, the young birds were on the wing.

We usually climbed down to our ravens' nest by a rope, when the young ravens were about three weeks old, and ringed them. In 1936 we lifted two from the five young birds in the nest, and reared them by hand. These became amusing pets for Ann, then six years old, who dubbed them Tinker and Inky. They were as full of mischief as a pair of boys at six years, and as soon as they learned to walk freely and use their wings they began to steal, play tricks, and tease in a delightful manner. The dog's tail and bare human legs were fatal attractions. The dog lost its temper very quickly and became sulky and retiring if the ravens appeared at a picnic. They had, indeed, a special fondness for picnic meals, but soon began carrying the joke too far: that is to say, from merely playing with food, silver spoons, forks, rings, eggs, and small articles, they took to flying off with these things, and losing or hiding them altogether.

It was time to shake them off and encourage them to go wild. In July and August, when ravens of this district become sociable and form quite large flocks of up to sixty individuals, young ravens from other nests wandered to the island, and Tinker and Inky joined them. Our precious pair gradually drifted away from us. Raven migration is probably very local; the young birds flock and roost together in the autumn, and probably remain vagrants until they have found a mate and a nesting site. The raven is now a numerous bird in Wales, where the sea-cliffs are its principal refuge, although many pairs nest on inland crags and on trees.

The very last we saw of Tinker and Inky was late in their first winter. For many weeks we had not had a visit from them. One day I saw a pair or ravens flying past at a height of about three hundred feet. I called my daughter's attention to them, and suggested that they might be her old pets. She ran over the grass and waved and shouted their names, whereupon they swerved from their course and stooped in unison, coming down to within a few feet of her head. One swift dip at her was all they made, then on they flew, leaving her delighted with this sign of recognition.

Ronald's other letters to his brother-in-law followed the same theme of identifying and observing the wildlife on the island.

The whole normality of the letters must have been a blessing to John. Ronald's naturalist writing was enlivened by his enjoyment, and love, of birds, animals, and indeed, people. All were described within the beautiful setting of Skokholm: rock-pipits and ravens, peregrines and puffins, the infernal and eternal problem of rabbits.

11

Inland Farm

(1943)

In 1940 Ronald Lockley was given notice by the War Office to evacuate Skokholm. To their sadness the family, together with the Baron, had to ferry their flocks, ponies and household and farming goods from the island to the Pembrokeshire mainland in September 1940. They found Inland Farm to rent, not far from Newport, a 'dilapidated old manor house', around the same size as Skokholm (around 240 acres), with numerous badgers, and otters in the river Nevern not far away.

It cost us well over £100 to transplant our roots from Skokholm to Inland Farm. But as a measure forced on us by the war it seemed, at the time, worth it. I had secured the farm at the low rent of £25 per annum for three years, with option to renew for a similar period at a rent to be fixed then by arbitration.

The farm was stated to be 200 acres, but there were over 30 acres of steep woodland, making about 165 acres of cultivatable land. A surveyor's report on its condition at the time of our entry revealed good reason for its nominal rent. The land was heavily deficient in lime. Each field had the same tale: 'Rabbits, bracken, thistles, needs the plough and half a ton per acre of basic slag.'

The same could have been said of Skokholm's fields when we entered the island in 1927. And we had never had the means to improve Skokholm.

Somehow this tough proposition was more fun to tackle than a smoothly running concern. One thing, we should have no time to pine for the island.

Anyway beggars cannot be choosers.

Inland Farm was almost as wild and inaccessible as Skokholm. It was once a 'gentleman's country residence'. It is described in a book written about 1800 as the 'only mansion hereabouts which has not been metamorphosed into a farmhouse'. It had then a lodge and a mile-long drive through the wooded valley. it had two wings, and, inside, panelled walls. It had two water-mills. It had an immense 'haggard' or stackyard, which was now empty, looking down towards the forecourt of the house.

The wooded drive had become choked and impassable, and you now reached the farm by way of a long, rough and precipitous road guaranteed to break your car's crown wheel and pinion if used often or at speed. At any rate it broke two crown wheels for me in as many months.

The east wing had long ago been pulled down, and the material used in the construction of a small bungalow, since converted into a useful implement shed.

Two fine oaks at the forecourt gate had also been pulled down, bringing sunshine to the little garden where the squire had once entertained summer parties on the lawn. The gateways had been upheaved by the roots of the trees, and gave the entrance a drunken look in keeping with the general neglect and rubbishy growth of nettles and weeds surrounding the house.

But the place had its possibilities, we decided. It had a fine rookery shading the house on the south side. A good coat of colour wash, an extra window or so where these had been walled in, would give it an air of being cared for. The forecourt would make an ideal herb garden, once its walls were restored and animals banned.

The slate room was sound enough, But underneath it existed that state known as 'indescribable' – paper and plaster coming down, fungi, damp, dirt, spiders and rats.

As for the land, most of the fields were level enough for two-way ploughing. The farm had had a great reputation, during the last war, for producing horses, cattle and corn. It was then paying £1 per day rent. But since those palmy days of high rents and higher farm prices it had gone down rapidly. It had had five tenants in as many years, each taking all he could away with him. And some of the best fields had been sold by the estate in order to keep out of debt.

It was a clear case for nationalization – good farm land which neither landlord nor tenant, for lack of capital, had succeeded in keeping up to the mark. It was disheartening, in war-time, to read and hear of its once-flourishing state, and to realise to what depths of dereliction private ownership and exploitation had reduced it.

Nationalization! That was the cure for all forms of badly managed private ownerships. And in a sense, as the farm was, it was said, about to be taken over by the Pembrokeshire War Agricultural Executive Committee – that is, the State – Inland Farm had been on the verge of becoming a nationalized property.

I had read all the leaflets issued by the Ministry of Agriculture, telling the farmer why and how he must apply for help if he felt he could not carry out the fullest possible programme of arable cultivations as outlined by his local District Cultivation Officer.

In my eagerness I agreed to carry out much more than the bare requirements of any cultivation order issued in respect of Inland Farm. I carefully read the leaflet issued by the Ministry explaining the Agricultural Requisites Scheme. I was reassured by the statement that I need 'have no misgivings' and that 'on being satisfied that your requirements are necessary for the food production campaign ... the Committee will get your requirements on your behalf.'

I was determined that I would have no misgivings.

I was determined to ask and go on asking for the maximum amount of help to get Inland Farm on its feet and producing food. The country wanted food, and we would produce it. I had only to say, with Churchill, 'Give us the tools and we will finish the job.'

It seemed to me that at last the Government was coming to its senses. In a properly ordered world the authorities should be able to say to the farmers: 'So many tons of this and that are needed to feed us all, here are the tools and the means, now go to it and produce exactly what we require, no less, and, if you can help it, no more.'

If only farmers had been told this in peace-time, and so avoided the bogey of over-production. But it had taken a second world war to bring a proper control of production, and it had come too late to be effective immediately, that is to say, when the nation needed it.

No wonder farmers were suspicious of the British Government's intentions! Ninety-nine per cent fully believe today that they are going to be let down after the war, that the old riot of uncontrolled markets and cheap imported food is going to ruin them as soon as peace is signed.

I include myself in the one per cent that hope and believe otherwise. But we shall only get a fair deal if we shout long enough about it.

These thoughts were in my mind constantly during the weeks in the autumn of 1940 when we were bringing our belongs up to the new farm, and gradually settling in. neighbouring farmers seemed to be ill-informed of the Government's plans to help the farmer to obtain credits and tools for his great task.

'You get it for me, they take no notice of me if I ask. You know how to write and demand it.'

'You're a plucky devil, tackling that farm and going straight for every kind of Government help. Keep it up and give 'em hell if they don't fulfil the promises they've made to us farmers.'

Thus my neighbours, interested in our experiment with derelict Inland Farm, and as ready to help me as to take advantage of any good I could do them, but suspicious of Government promises and Government credits. Typical hard-working and independent men who had had a tough struggle to keep their farms going during the years of peace and depression.

Mainland Farming, after the trials of farming in, and transport to, an island, seemed to have little difficulties except those of capital. And now the question of capital seemed to have been solved. Money had bothered but never impressed me. Money was the servant, not the master, of man.

Ronald prepared a list of requirements. He filled in a Requisites Scheme form requesting credits of £760 for seed potatoes and equipment for potato-growing, and £740 for growing oats, barley and clover, including lime, slag, artificial manures, seed corn and grass seeds, tractor fuel, and some animal feeding-stuffs. In all, £1,500 was requested. Ronald submitted the form, and waited.

There were a thousand interesting things happening every day. Mainland farming was full of surprises – not all of them good ones.

But we had been lucky over the tractor. The landlord had supplied his late bailiff with an oldish model Fordson tractor on pneumatics, plus a Ransome two-furrow plough, and a rather worn-out disc-harrow. These the bailiff had used to work and fallow some forty acres of foul land during the summer of 1940, a considerable help in my cropping programme, 1941. These I had been able to take over direct, the landlord promising to transfer ownership on payment of a round sum of £144, a very fair price at that time.

The three machines would do most of my cultivations. My neighbour offered me a damaged heavy tractor roller which the Baron said he could lick into shape.

Needing a farm horse and some cattle, Ronald went to some local sales. He bought several beef shorthorns, aiming to rear milking shorthorn calves with them. Then the Baron bought Jewel, a working mare, and Ronald bought other pieces of equipment for the farm at very low cost.

It was time we tried out the tractor. I had never driven one before. We oiled and greased and serviced her and then started her, without any difficulty. She roared away 'just like a typhoon', said the Baron. 'Typhoon' therefore was she named.

Without stopping her I hitched up the wagon with a borrowed tractor hitch and roared away at seven miles per hour. All went well until I was climbing the hill for home with a full load of feed. In changing from medium to low gear I failed to engage properly. It seems that a tractor must not be in motion when the gears are being changed. You should disengage the clutch, which, in a new tractor, acts as a brake and halts you; then you change gear.

Unfortunately the transmission or clutch brake mechanism was weak, and with a heavy load on the hill it could not hold the wagon. I ought, of course, to have changed to low gear before starting up the hill. Next time I certainly would – if there was to be a next time.

For the loaded wagon had now taken charge and was starting backwards down the precipitous hill, dragging the tractor with it.

Some woodmen witnessed the incident, and afterwards 'the talk was out' that I was lucky. I fumbled desperately with the gears and clutch, but in vain. Only the trailer wheels, swinging to the low roadside bank and being held there on the edge of an almost sheer drop into the valley, saved me.

The woodmen came up, and after a good deal of spade and shovel work we got the outfit straightened and linked up again. Then I resumed the ascent, crawling along in low gear until I was on level ground again.

When it came to threshing, neighbours came to help unasked, anxious to assist the stranger in their midst. In four hours we threshed out the lot, including nearly two tons of the oats brought from Newport. Most of the black oats I kept back unthreshed – I was told that these had a feeding value in the sheaf as good as good meadow hay.

Neighbour John's wife helped Doris to bring tea out to the machine at three o'clock, according to the custom of the district. As work was not urgent, the drum was stopped for twenty minutes while sat in the sun and ate and talked.

Doris had been alarmed at the number of neighbours reported to be coming to help our threshing. They would, of course, all require tea and supper. And as yet the house wasn't anywhere near straight. But good neighbour John had gathered together just sufficient to help and no more. And in fact, anxious not to overburden us, he had dropped hints among the workers that day, with the result that they had slipped away quietly. The Baron, Doris and I came in to a groaning supper-table alone.

It was rather a flat ending to a strenuous day.

By good chance I heard of a Welsh boy looking for a job as farm labourer, and went to see him at his home in one of the wooded cwms which cut through the farmlands in this district. Gwyn had been a rabbit-trapper, but now wished to become a labourer. A labourer could get exemption from the Armed Forces, and quite rightly, Gwyn knew he would make a better contribution to the war as a farm hand than as a soldier. I liked the frank way in which he said this.

But I must agree to let him trap the rabbits at Inland Farm, and this I was not very wiling to do. I have always hated the steel rabbit-trap, believing that it will never exterminate or even adequately control the rabbit. The Baron was doing very well with the ferrets which he had brought with him from the island.

But rather than lose Gwyn I agreed that he should make a first round or two with his traps at Inland Farm. Once the bulk of the rabbits were taken we could rely on ferreting and hedging for the rest. I hired Gwyn for one year, and agreed to pay a rent for the use of his rabbit-traps.

It was an excellent move. Gwyn was versed in all phases of local farming lore. He could plough and cultivate with tractor-powered implements, and right away we set up the Ransome two-furrow plough and got it working.

In a few days I was a ploughman. As soon as Gwyn had shown me how to open a field, and how to adjust the plough to the lie of the land, I sent him off to his trapping.

What a joy there is in ploughing! To me there was the same pleasure as in sailing. In the days of island life I could set my sails, trim my boat, tie the tiller, and then sit watching the water fly in silver curves from the bow as the little ship darted away before a fresh summer breeze.

But the two little curves of mould turning before the ploughshares gave a greater, deeper satisfaction. The mark made by the passage of a boat over the sea is fugitive, and remains only in the memory, but the passage of the plough is the turning of a page in the history of the field. The ploughman is making history – a very vital history as long as war lasts.

Early in November 1940, after several weeks of waiting for news of his application for financial assistance, Ronald Lockley was summoned to a meeting of the Pembrokeshire War Agricultural Executive Committee. The appointment was set for 11.30 am; he was not called in until 1.30 pm. Firstly he was told he had asked for far too much money; it was impossible; Ronald was to reduce his demands.

There ensued a long battle of wits between farmer and Committee in which Ronald laid out his well-planned scheme for growing potatoes, and the Committee argued that it was too ambitious. Ronald produced the leaflet which said: 'On being satisfied that your requirements are necessary for the food production campaign, the Committee will get your requirements on your behalf.' *But nobody on the Committee had seen the leaflet before. One member called it 'misleading'. Ronald left the meeting with no assurances of funding. He was told his case would be submitted to the Ministry and he would hear from them in a fortnight's time.*

After five weeks, Ronald wrote a desperate letter to the Minister of Agriculture. The funding and equipment were needed urgently – ground needed to be prepared for planting and winter was setting in.

No doubt I was unduly impatient, but I was angry that my time had been wasted, and I wasn't going to stand any more humbug about this Requisites Scheme. If the Government meant to help as stated in its leaflets, it must do so, and right up to the hilt. If not, then the whole thing should be exposed as a farce.

So it was in rather a bitter mood that I wrote a series of articles entitled 'Stories from a Derelict Farm' and sent them to the editor of the *Farmer and Stock-breeder*. It seemed to me that I could fulfil an important mission after all, in our mainland farming, quite apart from making derelict land produce food crops. There seemed to be an opening for a writer who would each week record his trials in getting the maximum assistance from the Government, who could publicly demand that the Ministry's promises be carried out. Only by a faithful record of our progress, published in a popular farming paper, would this be possible.

The editor of the *Farmer and Stock-breeder* agreed to publish the series. Subsequently he altered the title to 'Trials of a Land Improver', and under this heading the articles have since continued. Part of the material forming this book is taken, with the editor's permission, from these articles.

The first article, boldly but truthfully headed by the editor: 'My application for credits up to £1,500' was published on December 17th [1940]. It described the new farm and gave details of my application for help and the interview with the local W.A.E.C.

Whether by design or coincidence I do not know, but that day I received a phone message asking me to meet the W.A.E.C. two days later, to discuss my application again.

Somehow there was quite a different atmosphere in the Committee meeting this time. I was not required to wait a moment.

It was first of all explained to me that potato-sprouting trays were not admitted on the list of requisites, although nothing had been said about this at the first meeting.

That, and the fact that it was now pretty well too late for me to buy boxes and enough seed in time, seemed automatically to knock out my twenty-six-acres profit-making early potato scheme. If desired, the Committee said, they would provide seed for seven or eight acres of early potatoes, no boxes supplied. They advised me to risk no more than eight acres of this 'speculative' crop.

If I agreed to this, then for the rest they were prepared to grant the requisites for the grain-growing. What else could I do? I agreed.

The Committee proceeded to go into my cropping programme with great interest now. It was clear that they meant business at last. I was almost ashamed of my previous querulousness, and of the way I had forced my troubles on these conscientious men, when I saw how eager they appeared to be to ensure that I had got each field planned right. I was quite humbled by their keenness in discussing the right manures and varieties of seeds, as if they were farming it each man for himself.

But still my heart was heavy. I had hoped that I could make my farm an example of what could be done to win the war with derelict land plus the utmost Government help. But now, with the potato scheme crushed, the fire had gone out of the enterprise. Nothing was left, I felt, but a hollow core.

When we had finished, every field catered for, I filled up a fresh Requisites form. The Committee promised that it should go before the Ministry with their official blessing.

Work at Inland Farm proceeded. Discussions were held in the farmhouse kitchen between Ronald and his team – Doris, the Baron, Pauline, a landgirl, and Trevor, an eighteen-year-old who was waiting to join the R.A.F.

Although the Welsh boy Gwyn never attended these conferences, being too shy to offer his opinion in public, and handicapped in our company by the fact that he thought, and mostly preferred to speak, in Welsh, we knew we could rely on him. He was a worker from start to finish, and the only one of us thoroughly trained in local methods. There was nothing he could not do on the farm – he was ploughman, thatcher, horseman, cowman, shepherd, rabbit-catcher, hedger, mason, carpenter.

[In the spring of 1941] we were about to sow Parc Pen Castell, fourteen acres, with the useful black oat, when I got wind of a combine drill in the district. I waited a day in order to get this on the farm.

It was all very well for outsiders to talk of the beauty of hand-sowing, and horse cultivations, and the grand old ways and days of the Old Testament. Plenty of admirers of my 'island' books, having read of the simple life at Skokholm, imagined that I would still be a primitive man on the mainland. And expected to find me, like the pictures on calendars, striding over the furrows with a seed lip or an apron sack at my waist, broadcasting by hand over the eternal mother, Earth. Or walking, day after day, behind the plodding team.

The few that managed to find me out in my new home were disappointed. I was, they said, 'not a bit like what I had pictured from your books'. And I would reply that this mainland life was not a bit like the life we had lived in Skokholm.

Heavens, I would have given much in that first mainland spring to have been allowed to return to the salt wave and care-free life of the island! I thought with longing of the puffins arriving there just at this time; a great day of early spring that had always been. And of the peace and happy solitude of the flower-filled, bird-haunted island spring.

But here we were on a more exciting task. Over 100 acres ploughed and going down to wonderful crops. I must not grumble. Here was a fight worth fighting. Here was good, visibly effective, essential work well worth doing – feeding as many men and animals as the land might be capable of. I was compelled by order to plough and crop not less than fifty-eight acres of Inland Farm. But already we had got twice that amount under the plough.

So I had no time even to talk to my readers. To autograph a book and drink a cup of tea with them was still possible, but to stay and talk and put the world right as in peace-time was impossible. Those who could not jump on the tractor or stand on the footboard of the combine drill with me were left standing in the yard, admiring, wondering, or cursing.

Hideous in appearance and voice as the tractor was, compared with the curves of a horse, or the rhythm of the human body broadcasting over furrows, there was yet something splendid about Typhoon and the twenty or so mechanical horses which pounded inside her engine casing, ready at the slightest touch of the controls to tear open two perfect furrows, to pull a half-ton or heavier ring-roll over the land, to carry a drill from dawn to dusk without pause over the cleaned land, to obey as blindly as a dog, and to respond to kindness and care and proper 'servicing' as readily as a stable of horses, but with less trouble and with greater efficiency.

'Greater efficiency' – yes, how the land screamed out for greater efficiency, greater attention, greater love, greater respect! Once upon a time this farm had been efficient, had carried something like twelve trained labourers and five teams of horses to its 360 acres. Now, its acreage almost halved, it carried one tractor, one horse, three young men, and old man and a land-girl. This was the minimum team compatible with spring-sowing efficiency for 100 or so acres, plus livestock and rabbit control duties. And we should not have got through the sowing with even moderate efficiency without the combine drill.

What a beautifully-made thing this combine drill was! If only man had confined his engineering genius to devising the constructive and labour-saving side. Instead he had spent, was now spending, almost all his energies upon the invention of death-dealing machines, more and more powerful, more and more horrible, more and more insane. We farmers still sowed seed to feed our children, and unborn generations, while the rest of the world was locked in a mad fight for 'freedom', that is to say in a terrible struggle to be rid of a monetary system rotten with false values.

Peasants all over Europe, and even along the bombarded Kentish shore, filled in shell craters, buried the slaughtered men and beasts, and sowed seed that man and beast might live again. That sowing, all sowing, was an act of faith that held in it a sweet, sad triumph and a new hope for the weary human spirit.

At the end of March the chiffchaff was singing in the bare boughs, soon to be followed by the willow-warbler with his undulating verse of soft sweet notes. So much of the wood had been cut down, leaving only the rookery and the hedgerow trees, that when the wood-warbler returned at the end of April he found his habitat so altered that he remained only a short while. For a week we heard his tragic bell notes and wind-like shivering song, then he retreated to some nearby glen where tall oaks still grew untouched by man and in number enough to give him sufficient singing and nesting territory.

The chaffinches were nesting in almost every sapling and bush – they were as plentiful as sparrows were scarce. A cock pied flycatcher had settled in a tree on the western edge of the rookery, and you could go out any day in April and May to listen to his sort, sharp shower of metallic notes, and glimpse his white and black livery in the wave-wind of the oak leaves. We did not see his mate at all – perhaps he was a novice lover, and failed to get a wife in his first summer.

The birds of this district of low tableland farms and deep-scoured, wooded valleys were interesting, contrasting favourably with the common birds which as a boy I had known in the orderly villages of Glamorganshire and Monmouthshire. Thus, house-sparrows are very scarce in the villages and farms of north Pembrokeshire – only on rare occasions would a pair visit Inland Farm. Even at harvest time you could not find a single sparrow among the yellow-hammers, chaffinches, linnets, goldfinches and greenfinches which visited the stubbles. Starlings were even scarcer than sparrows as breeders, although they wintered in immense flocks from October to March.

Goldfinches were more numerous than greenfinches, yellow-hammers more plentiful than wood-pigeons, missel-thrushes more abundant than song-thrushes, woodlarks more common than skylarks. None was happier than I in recognizing these unusual ornithological circumstances. From the fruit-grower's point of view the comparative scarcity of the blackbird and the song-thrush was not to be too greatly deplored – there were barely enough of these birds to strike a persistent note in the dawn chorus. As it was, at times you had to go out of your way to hear a blackbird singing. I could not quite understand why they should be so scarce; possibly many were killed in the rabbit-traps which had exterminated so much of the rare forms of wild life: a blackbird was all too ready to investigate the fresh earth laid over a gin-trap set in the hedgerow, or, as often happened, illegally set in the open.

You could not regret unduly the fact that only one lark in every five singing in the summer sky was a skylark. The other four were woodlarks. A tamer, more friendly, sweeter-voiced singer is the woodlark, his passion less wild and ringing, more homely than that of the skylark, more like the bells of a cathedral ringing in the soft distance of a far-off valley. The stump-tailed woodlarks would rise before me from the grass of the fields, flutter in a hovering flight, then soar up singing or settle back quickly to earth with quiet, tinkling notes.

The damp wood of the Rhos, at the top of the farm, was the haunt of many kinds of forest birds. Bullfinches, green and pied and barred woodpeckers, nuthatches, tree-creepers, tree-pipits, ring-doves, blackcaps, whitethroats, willow-warblers, and great, coal, marsh, blue, and long-tailed tits. Buzzards, kestrels and brown owls nested there. Wild ducks and moorhens had sanctuary in its boggy acres, and sedge-warblers prattled in the overgrown thickets.

Beneath the trees and in the wet open glades were many kinds of orchids.

This was our first spring for many years on the mainland, and, between the rush of farming work, we enjoyed its soft, tree-bowered loveliness as a great contrast to the vivid spring on the naked island of Skokholm.

Also during 1941, Ronald Lockley got involved in a new project – the growing of flax. This was used for canvas, aeroplane fabric, hose-pipes, parachute harness, and fine rope. The idea was 'sold' as an urgent need because of the war, but also as a long-term crop for the linen trade. Ronald proposed growing twelve acres of flax, but was asked to increase it to twenty acres. He was also promised enough potash to prepare the soil. Frustration, however, was to ensue.

Flax, said the circular dealing with its cultivation, needs an onion-bed tilth. It must not be sown after April 15th at latest.

But when April 15th arrived with no sign of the flax seed or the manures, I could delay no longer. The twenty acres of tilled land had already started a crop of weeds while waiting for the flax seed. Three days later the weather was dry enough for us to harrow these weeds out. The sun scorched them up, and in the next two days I drilled the land down with oats.

At the end of April a lorry entered the gates of the farm. It was carrying a ton of flax seed. No apologies, no explanation from the driver, who was merely carrying out his orders as employee of a road haulage contractor. Nor did the driver have any knowledge of the whereabouts of our ton of potash.

I sent the driver down to the kitchen for a cup of tea while I thought the problem out. This was one of the moments when the telephone, which, when it rang at night after a weary day, I would curse from the sleepy comfort of my armchair before the log fire, came into its own. I rang through the manager of the factory, got him just in time, and asked him what I was to do with flax seed. I had already, I complained, sown down to oats the land saved for the flax. What the dickens did he take me for, sending seed up here two weeks behind the final date for sowing?

'For God's sake,' came the reply, 'try to put it in, late or not. The seed deliveries have been far behind schedule, due to a thousand and one things beyond my control. Do your best – we need every thread of flax to arm the fighting services.'

'But where is the potash?'

'God knows!' He put down the receiver.

After a conversation with the chief cultivations officer for the W.A.E.C. Ronald and Pauline sowed the flax seed in the only available meadow, Parc Ysgubor, which first had to be ploughed and got ready, which took three days. The flax grew, and was harvested with the help of a team of fifty Royal Marines, who arrived at the end of September. The crop brought in a total of £360 – a profit of around £300 in the first season. Ronald was then appointed to recruit growers of flax in the north of Pembrokeshire, alongside his work at Inland Farm.

Ronald then got drawn into a new scheme for making silage, which was successful.

As a writer in the farming press, I was expected to set a good example in war-time, said my advisor, Fuller Lewis. I pointed out that the title of my contributions was 'Trials of a Land Improver' – not Triumphs.

'You'll find that triumphs and trials are one and the same indistinguishable thing in farming,' Fuller went on. 'Now what about this straw-pulp plant?'

'Straw-pulp?'

'The conversion of straw from an indigestible bulky fill-belly to a valuable and easily assimilated food equal to good hay and roots.'

We discussed the arrangements for a silage and straw-pulp demonstration at Inland Farm, to be held under the auspices of the War Agricultural Executive Committee. For this purpose the Government, in conjunction with the benevolent agricultural policy of Imperial Chemical Industries Ltd, was to defray the cost of erecting a straw-pulp plant at Inland Farm. It was doubtful if we had enough water to keep a straw-pulp plant going in the summer – it needed at least 150 gallons of water an hour – but a straw-pulp plant was normally not required except in the winter when there is water in plenty on most farms.

The weather on demonstration day was fine, the sky cloud-free, and hay-making was going forward on a dozen farms in sight of Inland Farm. Still there were plenty of people anxious to see what was going forward on this once almost derelict farm, where land, producing last year barely three tons of oats, had now 120 acres under cultivation. It was advertised as an 'after-tea' demonstration. The crowd came from 6 p.m. onwards, and Fuller Lewis gave an illustrated lecture about the straw-pulping process.

'And now', said neighbour Thomas, 'three cheers for R. M. Lockley, who, by his articles on the trials of the farmer, has done us a lot of good in Pembrokeshire, and who, by his generosity, has thrown open the gates of Inland Farm to all comers, at all times ready to help and be helped. There was a day in my youth when it was an honour to enter this old farm, and come into this old yard – and that was the day of the family James, who farmed it like a clock, like a calendar. But in late years it has gone from bad to worse, and from worse to the devil, until for very shame and sadness no farmer who knew it of old has cared to go near.

'I declare to you all now that it's done my heart good today to come here and see every field bearing the marks of good husbandry, of honest work and endeavour, the house clean with a bright wall-wash, the gardens set with flowers and vegetables fit to shame even an old farmer and gardener like myself. There's many of us here today have learnt much besides this business of silage and straw-pulp, which some of us perhaps think is a lot of old nonsense. I mention no names, but I'll say this: it's the farmers who don't find time to attend demonstrations that need the most teaching, and more than likely the most of us here will profit from what we've seen.'

'Aye, and I'll second that!' said neighbour John. 'I'll second three cheers for Lockley and his courage in tackling the old place. I know a bit about Inland Farm, for I had a year at it myself and was glad to quit. That was before the war. But what I like about Lockley is his writing about his failures just as much and more than about his successes. And I like the way he's trying all the things we other too cautious farmers dare not – silage and straw-pulp and flax. So, here's to wish him and his hard-working wife every success in the future. Hip hip hooray!'

Looking around in desperation I tried to think of some diversion. But the cheers were followed by demands for the inevitable speech. Up I had to go, upon the wagon.

'Ladies and gentlemen,' I stammered, 'I gladly take this opportunity to thank you for coming here today, and to say how much I have appreciated your kindness shown to my wife and me, who are south Pembrokeshire folk, English-speaking like all south-county people, and therefore foreigners to you. Would that I could speak in Welsh, but wisely perhaps my right-hand man Gwyn never got further than teaching me the few simple words which you say in Welsh when you hit your thumb with a hammer. I see among you today some of those warm-hearted people whom I did not know at the time, but who, soon after we arrived here, showed us the strength of the good neighbourship which binds this district together.

'The first neighbour to call came from quite far away – too far for me easily to repay his kindness. He carried a sack of potatoes, and he said that he thought we would very likely be short in this our first winter. Nor did he disclose his name, wanting rather to do good without thought of repayment. I only learned his name much later, when I met him at Eglwyswrw Fair. Another neighbour loaned me a horse, a third a cart and some harness. Yet another sent his son and a plough along. All of you called on me to ask me not to hesitate to request your help when I needed it. And your wives have helped mine to fit into your ways and learn your pleasant customs.'

I now called upon other farmers to thank Fuller Lewis for

his day of advice, entertainment, and hard work. Then: 'Let all who are thirsty and hungry go to the old kitchen for such refreshment as is provided.'

Most of the farmers, knowing the difficulties of catering for such a crowd in war-time, moved off. But the odd labourers, roadmen, and others who had no expectation of ever making silage or straw-pulp for themselves, trailed down to the kitchen. This, for them, was the real and essential part of demonstration day.

For a month in early summer, 1941, Ronald was on the sea again for the Royal Navy, but his activities were not elaborated on in this book, published in 1943, during hostilities. He was thrilled to be back at sea. Shortly after that, back at Inland Farm, there came the possibility of farming Island Farm as well, and thoughts of starting a co-operative farming venture.

12

The wartime co-operative farm
(1942–1943)

RML's columns had been read by many, and here with Ronald and Doris, early in 1942, were nine of his readers, all keen to start on a farming adventure in Pembrokeshire. They were to work both Inland Farm and the newly obtained Island Farm on Dinas Head, between Fishguard and Newport. Together, one Sunday morning, they all walked the eight miles from Inland Farm to Island Farm, to survey their forthcoming project.

Cyrus was fifty-three, and had brought his wife Teresa, their twenty-year-old twins Lorry and Lydia, and £50. Their home in Coventry had been bombed. 'The Baron' was seventy, and an old friend of Ronald's. Tommy Austin was twenty-eight, and alone in the world, after his new wife, a nurse, had died in the Dunkirk evacuation. He too had been injured, and invalided out of the Army. He came with £1000. Pauline and Celia were Women's Land Army volunteers. And there was Timothy Players too, a forty year-old smallholder. All of them believed that co-operative farming was the future.

The west way to the farm was no more than a track of potholes in the slate rock; it was sunk down into the land and almost too narrow for a wide cart to pass. Where it began, by the sea's edge, it was smothered in a drift of dry sand blown by the incessant west wind.

"Is this the only road to Island Farm?" I asked a lone

fisherman on the beach, more for the sake of conversation than for information. I had a large-scale map in my pocket and knew that there was another road. The fisherman told us that it was much worse than the west road. The east way, he said, was just a mud track through a shut-in wooded valley. Once it had been a cart-track, but a cloudburst had washed it away, leaving nothing but a slippery clay gutter.

"I suppose you're not thinking of taking the farm, are you?" the white-moustached fisherman asked anxiously, staring curiously at the assembled co-operators.

"And if we were?"

"I'd advise you not to be so stupid. Pardon me, but it's never been any good since the Owens left. The road was in fair condition then. But it's been washed out since. Island Farm's like that – you suffer half the year by floods, and the rest of the time it's a scorching drought. It's broken too many good men and stout hearts. D'you come from these parts?"

"Eight miles away. Inland Farm. I myself want to get back to the sea. I'm a fisherman at heart, too."

There were plenty of lobsters here, he said, and some salmon and bass. Oh, yes, and plenty of mackerel and herring and pollack. We began to discuss nets. If I brought with me my trammel net he would be willing to show me the best places . . .

He even relented a bit about Island Farm. If we got our crops in really early all would be well. The winter moisture would be in the ground. If we got enough of that to make our straw, we'd get our corn certain. The best place for corn in the county. And early harvest would save the autumn rains. Early sown, early mown, the saying was. But on the whole, it was too difficult in its present condition, nearly every field full of brambles, thorns, furze and rubbish. Only one or two fields around the house fit to walk in.

He was horrified to learn that if we found the place suitable we were going to crop it that year. It was already February and nothing ploughed. No one dared take the place even in September, with all the winter to do the work in. How much more foolish of us to think of taking it in the spring! The War Agricultural Executive Committee had advertised for months and months but failed to obtain a suitable tenant. But, of course, he grinned, I was only joking?

In the rutty lane partridges were calling. There were yellow-hammers singing from the glowing spikes of the gorse as we moved up the road to the farm. A charm of goldfinches circled around, then settled back to feed on the seeds of the weeds in the steep roadside banks. The rosettes of the foxgloves filled the spaces between the furze bushes. The leafless trailers of honeysuckle and wild roses were wreathed in confusion everywhere.

Already a deep satisfaction was taking the place of the feeling of surprise within me. And the exclamations from the rest showed that they, too, were feeling happy.

From its dirt bath in the pathway a brown bird with a short tail fluttered, shaking the dust from its freckled plumage. It rose in a shallow spiral. I recognized the woodlark, and wondered at finding such a bird on a bare peninsula.

Suddenly it began to pour out its rich bell-like song.

For a while we all watched it; myself still surprised that a bird of wooded hill country should be living on this naked coast. What a grand song! I had always loved the woodlark. Its song, its friendliness, its rarity, combined to make it lovable. Curious how these small things mattered so much to me – much more than the richness of the farm or its prospects of financial success.

The lane broke into a huge stackyard – it was three acres in extent – grass-grown, devoid of any rick or stack. In the lowermost corner were the farmhouse and buildings, tucked down out of view in a manner characteristic of many Welsh farms. A background of trees and fields, but with the front door facing the muck-yard. Most of the buildings showed large gaps in their ancient, slated roofs, or else were entirely roofless, their slates half blown away and their timbers rotting and green with mould.

A quick glance round the deserted buildings convinced us of the great difficulties as well as the possibilities. The stable, granary, barn, calves' and pigs' cots were without roofs, and their dirt and cobble floors were rat-ridden and filthy. The once elaborate water-wheel mechanism was broken and scattered, and the wheel itself missing. Everywhere was neglect and decay, and, to one used to the movement of animals about farm buildings, a dreary silence and the cold stink of fungi and death in place of the warm reek of animals and their droppings.

Two buildings only had sound roofs, one of corrugated iron, the other of asbestos tiles, both recently built and fitted with enough glass to make two long, indifferently lighted potato-chitting sheds. The last farmer had pinned his faith in the production of early potatoes, and had gone to some expense to provide sprouting houses. But apparently he had not gone far enough to satisfy the War Agricultural Executive Committee who had taken the farm and advertised it to let.

As a bait to prospective tenants, the W.A.E.C. offered to repair the house and buildings sufficiently to enable a man to farm the island properly. They would provide a water supply and other facilities within reason as required for the farmer's special purpose. All expenditure above the initial cost (stated to be £150, a most inadequate sum, we were to find; it should have been £500) of repairing the buildings would be capitalized at 5 per cent, and this interest would be added to the farmer's rent, which was to be £140 per annum. This rent had been arrived at by arbitration between the owner and the W.A.E.C.

The whitewashed, slate-roofed house was outwardly not in bad repair. Its walls and two main roofs were sound. Inside, the owner's wife and family were on the point of packing up and quitting. We were shown over the house, a long building inconveniently planned with four rooms in a row and a dairy at the back on the ground floor, and eight rooms of varying size above. The kitchen was badly lighted, and had a broken-down and inadequate cooking stove. There was no water laid on. Water had to be fetched from a well across the boggy wooded valley behind the house. There were signs of rats in every room. The outdoor sanitation consisted of the usual sentry-box over a gutter which relied on being flushed only when heavy rains gathered enough water from the back roof of the house. It would then be flushed, or partly flushed, into the stream in the valley; but this, I was told, often went dry in the summer. So many Welsh farms adopt this practice of setting up the closet over running water; more particularly does the insanitary custom prevail in isolated mountain districts where one would expect to find streams unpolluted.

No, on the whole, you could not ask self-respecting people to go into that farmhouse and make a home there in its present condition. But where were we to house all our workers?

Island Farm was 438 acres in area, of which 89 was stated to be pasture, 71 arable, 23 fallow, 56 reclaimable, 156 rough grazing, 11 marsh, 7 acres house and woodland, and the rest waste land and cliff margins.

From the house and yard a track led up through the empty fields to the abandoned ruin of a coastguard hut on the very top of the island at 463 feet above sea-level. We made our way slowly through the thistle and bracken-infested land. The farther you moved away from the yard the wilder the fields became, until in the big field of thirty-five acres at the top of the farm you were walking by rough paths through bramble, furze and blackthorn, growing above your head. Here was a perfect paradise for rabbits and wild birds and small creatures. Larks, stonechats, blackbirds, thrushes, dunnocks and yellow-hammers made up the population of winter birds. Kestrels and sparrow-hawks and buzzards hunted for rodents and small life. No doubt in the summer there were plenty of bush warblers to swell the dawn chorus. The warm slope looked as if it would suit adders and lizards too.

The naturalist in me had no wish to disturb this sanctuary. In peace-time, with a little judicious planting of berry-bearing bushes and evergreens, such a sanctuary could have been made complete. But today I was looking upon the scene with a farmer's eye, planning how best the land would pay. The soil here was good, a rich loam full of humus, and considering the height of the field, very free from rock and stone, more so than some of the lower fields. The plough would have to come here, after the bush had been uprooted and burnt. No ordinary plough could tackle land with such an ancient root system. A caterpillar tractor and a wide, heavy single-furrow plough of the 'prairie-buster' type would be necessary.

RML had three seemingly insurmountable problems when he first took over Island Farm: rats, rabbits, and lack of accommodation. Rabbit-catching was a lucrative job in those days when food production was so important to the war effort – so lucrative, in fact, that it seems that rather than trying determinedly to eradicate them, the trappers would try to leave rabbits on the land to breed – so that they could provide the trappers with income the following season! They also used gin-traps, which also caught stoats and weasels – the natural enemy of the rabbit. The trapper admitted that stoats were, then, extinct in Pembrokeshire because of the gin-trap, and said that before the introduction of use of the gin-trap there were few rabbits – because of the stoats and weasels.

The rats were a disgusting, omnipresent, and insanitary pest and needed to be dealt with urgently. Ronald brought in a fleet of cats.

For accommodation, Ronald managed to call at a house in Cwm-yr-Eglwys, the hamlet just below Island Farm, just as the previous tenants had left, and so the Neat House became home to Cyrus, Teresa, Lydia, Ronald and Doris (Ann was away at school), while Timothy, Tommy and Lorry were to farm Inland Farm with the help of Celia and Pauline.

The next morning Cyrus and his family accompanied Ronald, walking, driving the sheep from Inland Farm to Island Farm – around eight miles. Cyrus and Ronald debated land reform – Cyrus was a Communist who believed in total State control of farms. Although Ronald believed in 'a gradual nationalisation', after a few hours he admitted that there was something in what Cyrus said about nationalising farming without delay.

It was an interesting time for Ronald. He'd been farming in Wales for years and knew the Welsh ways of doing things, and what 'did well' and what was chancy. He was suddenly face to face with younger people who wanted progress, and older people who had farmed in England and considered English ways far superior to Welsh ways. Ronald wanted a 'co-operative' farm, so he had to co-operate with all of them. He seems to have succeeded by telling them that although he disagreed with them, but in the end it was up to them. Sometimes their English ways were taken up (and sometimes they succeeded), and sometimes they bowed to Ronald's experience.

At Island Farm, Ronald decided to grow flax (required for making canvas, aeroplane fabric, hose-pipes, parachute harness, fine rope and so on), with which he'd done well at Inland Farm – the seed was delivered free, and there was a payment once it had been sown. Rye was another crop – the Ryvita Company offered similar terms for growing it. Then there was the farm's quota of wheat to grow, and barley too, and oats grown from the farm's own seed. They also grew potatoes. All this was required to help wartime food supplies. Timothy wanted to grow tomatoes and veg. Lorry was keen on growing maize and tobacco.

Rye was a new crop in Pembrokeshire. If it was all that the Ryvita Company claimed for it, it would be a profitable crop. It grew in bad ground and needed no fertilizer. The Company supplied the seed at a low figure, and for this they railed it free and dressed with a mercurial powder which prevented, or at least minimized, various diseases such as bunt, smut, ergot and leaf-stripe. And they guaranteed to buy the crop back at the price fixed by the Government for feed rye.

The Baron knew all about rye. He had grown it in the north-west – Alberta. Easy as winking to grow. You could crop it green at first and then let it run up into a straw crop. Its straw was the finest in the world for thatching, made marvellous house-roofs, barn-roofs, cattle-kraals. Yes, sir, we'd be wise guys if we grew rye; only we must seed it thick, insisted the Baron, we must not hunk with it, at least 4½ bushels to the acre.

The Ryvita Company recommended 3 bushels to the acre. We compromised and sent an order for 3½ bushels of seed rye to the acre.

Ryvita Ltd. executed the order at once. The seed arrived [at the railway station] a few days later. But our lorry had not yet arrived; and the station lorry could not, would not, and did not deliver it. There was no lorry on hire locally. We might have fetched it with a tractor and trailer; but the station was nine miles away, and we had not yet had delivery of the two trailers ordered from the local coachbuilder-blacksmith.

The W.A.E.C. was now approached. Yes, the machinery department would hire a lorry. We could have it tomorrow, and keep it until our new lorry arrived from the Fordson works. Next day Tommy and I went in to fetch the lorry from the depot, only to meet an adamant assistant executive office who refused to release it. The executive officer was away, and the machinery officer had been reprimanded for agreeing to its release. No, sir, he, the assistant executive officer, had no power even in an emergency such as I represented our need to be, to release a lorry.

Probably he was carrying out the letter of the petty laws by which he was governed, but here we had come twenty-six miles in good faith to pick up the promised lorry. Four five-ton lorries stood idle outside the W.A.E.C.'s store, and four drivers sat smoking cigarettes, awaiting orders. At last one lorry went down to the station, half a mile away, and fetched a parcel of bolts which were light enough to be carried under your arm. But all that afternoon, while Tommy and I raged, and nearly seized and drove a lorry away in despair, the other three lorries stood bound up in red tape.

So we went home, a wasted day and a wasted car ride of fifty-two miles behind us.

My note of protest to the executive officer brought a message late that night that a lorry and driver were coming up to us next morning, on hire at 7s 6d per hour. We used that lorry, but we were not allowed to drive it, though Tommy was an expert driver. A succession of physically unfit drivers, W.A.E.C. employees exempt from military service, drove for us – whenever they remembered to arrive on time, or at all. They would drive their empty lorry to their sometimes far-distant home each night, thus wasting more valuable time and fuel. They drove into gateposts, and got as deeply stuck in fields as their superiors were in Whitehall regulations.

Such were some of the trials of the exasperated farmer, dealing with a red-tape-bound W.A.E.C.

Rabbits, rats, and mice were still a huge problem for Ronald at Island Farm, but he was enjoying getting to know the wildlife of the place.

There were several badger earths or setts in the surrounding woods, but I found that this creature did little damage to corn, apparently seldom trampling in it but preferring to hunt slugs, snails, worms, beetles, small mammals, roots and wild fruits which made up its food, along the edge of the rye, in the rough corners, in woods, and over rocky waste land.

The badgers obviously did more good than harm. They destroyed the destroyers of the corn. They were part of the balance of nature in the field, part of the wild feet and wings which played the game on the side of man. The other allies were the weasels – still a few saved from the traps – the brown owls living in the wood and subsisting much on rats and mice, and one pair of white owls, probably living in a cave on the cliffs, and the little owls nesting in holes in the trees or the hedge. By day there were the hovering kestrels and buzzards to take toll of the rodents. There was a deep joy for me in the sight of the beautiful russet-red-backed kestrel hanging motionless over the little paths on the edge of the field, quartering with his sharp eye each section of the hedge, then suddenly diving with outstretched talons upon his prey. The buzzard often hovered too, or slowly beat the field with broad, noiseless, golden wings, before dropping on unsuspecting rodent, insect or lizard.

As summer wore on I was delighted to hear nightjars crooning in the adjacent spit of rough wood, rock, bracken and furze. On quiet summer evenings I stole through the fern, anxious to watch these night-hawking birds at play. With wild, twisting flight and clapping wing they darted through the edge of the wood, now swinging out over the corn in pursuit of moths and cockchafers, now suddenly alighting on a branch or in the pathway. Many times they settled on the bare ground of the farmyard, probably, I thought, in order to pick up grit to aid digestion of their chitinous diet of insects.

The web of life over and on and under the rye-field was an intricate one. The nightjars fed on cockchafers and daddy-long-legs and other noxious insects whose grubs lived under the ground eating the tender roots of the corn.

Dozens of small warblers fringed the rye-field, feeding on caterpillars, flies, grubs, spiders and other insects, noxious, neutral and beneficial to man. In one part of the field I frequently disturbed a pair of woodlarks. The male hovered over the field at a height of about one hundred and fifty feet, pouring out his rich, bell-like song. But as the corn became ripe he grew silent, and it was only at rare moments now that I put up the pair with their family of four stub-tailed larklings. In another part of the field skylarks nested. Both kinds of lark were beneficial to the rye.

So the ecological web of life in the rye-fields at high summer grew more absorbing the more I studied it. As the grain ripened and hardened a few birds came to pull at the ears. There were no sparrows on the farm, and the handful that lived in the hamlet were of no consequence – in fact I do not recollect seeing them on the rye at all. But linnets, chaffinches, greenfinches and yellow buntings stole a few grains. When the rye was cut, rooks, jackdaws, and crows and gulls came to settle on the sheaves and fill their crops, but never in such numbers as to alarm us. A shot from a gun now and then would keep them away for a day – it was clear they were not hungry for rye; they had other sources of food at that season.

After harvesting the rye and the flax, it was time to stack it all. Now, the differences in farming methods between England and Wales became apparent once again.

We had threshed out the thirteen-acre field, and were starting on the six-acre field, with the straw pile built up into a huge, square, hollow-topped mass, by noon on the third day. We were about to lay off for dinner when someone noticed a huge storm-cloud gathering over the mountains and moving in our direction.

The principle of building very large straw stacks and hay ricks is an English one; it is dictated by convenience, large fields and fair harvest weather. Our co-operators were English born and bred farm-workers, believing in English methods. But in Wales we like to put our hay and corn and straw in several small ricks and stacks. We thus avoid the danger of overheating, and we can always top up quickly a small stack for the night or against the threat of a storm. Now we had already built immense flax stacks from the fifty acres we had grown on this farm, and several times rain had caught us napping. At that moment all our canvas rick-sheets were in use covering, not very adequately either, our flax stacks until we should have time to thatch them.

There was not a stitch of canvas left to cover the great table of the rye straw, nor was there a possibility of our topping up the centre in time. Desperately we worked to fill up the great hollow in the centre of this stack. Had I not begged the co-farmers to "keep the centre up" when building stacks and ricks? It was much easier, they considered, to build a flat rick and top it up afterwards, but it is a fatal policy, as the lower horizontal or inward-inclining sheaves let in as much water as those similarly wrongly positioned do on top. Some of the stacks built that summer were topped with sheaves with their outer edges higher than their inner ends; so the rain ran downhill into, not out of, the stack.

Eagerness to get the job quickly was a phase which was strong in the first year of co-farming. And constantly to advise and warn and admonish was not easy in these early days – at least I found it difficult, fearing the blunt the friendly atmosphere of our co-partnership. But it was to lead to some very bitter lessons.

One of the first was on the day of that magnificent but disastrous thunderstorm. A dense, black, columnar cloud seemed to rise like the smoke of a volcano out of the top of the highest mountain in the south-east. At first it was attenuated and surrounded by patches of blue sky. We made bets that it would pass us by. But soon a new black host was uprising from all the mountains of our southern horizon. The sun and the sky became quickly veiled with ever-thickening cloud.

There was a cool rush of air. Over us hung the indigo belly of the largest storm-cloud I have ever seen.

One contorted lane of vivid lightning was suddenly outlined against this great blackness; then, before the thunder came, the centre of the sky seemed to crack.

A flood was fallen upon us. In two or three seconds everyone was wet through. In two or three minutes great rivers of brown water were leaping and playing down the cart ruts leading to the rye-field, and spreading out in a broad sheet over the grass and the stubble. In ten minutes the rye-straw stack was wet through, and water streamed from the very bottom.

Two days later we resumed operations. Somehow the water had seeped down and out through the lightly packed straw, leaving the top part fairly dry. A fresh wind helped. There was nothing to do but hope for the best, and build on top of the sunken stack. At least the straw was by nature too hollow and dry to heat – though it might go musty.

After this, the co-operators paid more attention to Ronald's experience of Welsh farming practices!

The co-operators decided to abide by the set of rules for governing an agricultural co-operative friendly society set down in the Industrial and Provident Societies Act 1893. Some new people had arrived, and they met to decide on an executive committee for running Inland and Island Farms. Apart from deciding on the chairman (Ronald), two farm managers (Cyrus and Tommy), and a secretary (Timothy), and a lot of hard talking about future developments, Tommy announced that the three 'lonely bachelors', Lorry, Timothy, and himself, ought to be allowed to see more of Celia, Pauline, and Jill – the Land Army volunteers: 'Could they come over on wash-days?'!

The work went on. The Ministry of Agriculture requested a record seeding of the pastures in 1942; this was achieved. But the long hours and days of work began to affect the workers.

In mid-May, the executive committee began to discuss the question of a holiday. This question had been forced on us. For some time danger signals had been hoisted. Every one of us had lost pounds in weight, and run into minor accidents of one sort or another through loss of poise and temper due to overwork and insufficient sleep in the wild rush to complete the spring work. Cyrus seriously alarmed us by going to bed for a fortnight with shingles. Pauline and

Tommy developed bad "tractor coughs", due to long hours over the fumes from tractor exhausts, and had to rest and do only the lightest work away from the tractors.

As soon as the last field was sown we arranged a week's holiday for everyone, to be taken in shifts so as to leave enough to manage the stock. Pauline and Lydia decided on a hitch-hike to London, to do, as they put it, some "shows" as a change from the country. They carried an introduction to Lord Perry, who showed them over the Fordson Co-operators' Estates, the Henry Ford Agricultural Institute, and the tractor works at Dagenham. The Baron, my wife and I sailed in the *Storm-Petrel* to the island sea-bird sanctuaries off the west coast. We camped out at Skokholm, seeing the myriads of puffins, guillemots, razorbills, and gulls by day, and hearing the wild cries of the petrels at night.

Like many other war workers in that hard spring of 1942 we had overworked, and we had nearly bust our little community in the doing. The time had come when we must have more fun and entertainment to balance our lives properly. Sensible entertainment: singing, decent music, healthy games and dancing.

We elected an entertainments committee with the rosy-faced Teresa as secretary. This move was a great success. Once a week we all met for this social evening at the Neat House. First there would be good music as the people gathered – either from the radio or from gramophone records brought by members. It was surprising how much of the music of the classical composers was available in our joint record library. When enough people were assembled we broke into fun with a Paul Jones dance, in which each changed his partner at a break in the music. Then followed games, charades, tricks, interspersed with dancing, especially to the lovely waltzes of Strauss. A light 'promenade' supper was served at ten o'clock, the cost of which was met by a levy of 3d. per head. Discussion on the farm work often broke out during this meal. While the cups and plates were being washed up the dancing continued. At eleven o'clock another log was thrown on the wide hearth in the big room, and the lights were switched off.

A huge semi-circle was formed – it was usually so full that it bulged out against the three walls of the room – and in the firelit glow we sang until midnight the old traditional songs. Some of our neighbours, boys and girls whose daily language was Welsh, had by now started part-time work with us; they and their friends added their glorious voices to our amateur choir. Often they would sing solo in Welsh.

It was a timely thing, this ritual of entertainments each week. No longer was there talk among the younger ones of time off for a trip to town, to the cinema and the dance-hall – this was replaced by light-hearted reminiscing over the last 'social' at the Neat House, and a discussion as the programme for the next.

And so we learned to join with our serious co-operative working for a living a comradeship of laughter and music and dancing, by which a more balanced and satisfying existence was created.

In the spring of 1942, Ronald Lockley set off on a new project – getting more farmers in Pembrokeshire to grow flax. This he had to do whilst also supervising his two farms. This left the co-operators doing most of the work, and Ronald working all day and most of the night. RML had spent a lot of his time in the English-speaking south of Pembrokeshire; this new job involved travelling round farms in the north of the county, meeting the resistance – and the hospitality – of the Welsh-speaking farmers there, and finding out about the life of the hill-farmer. They were not traditionally experimentalists! By the end of February 1943, Ronald had coaxed only fifteen farmers to grow flax, which, including Ronald's own flax, would make up only three-fifths of the quota for the county. By mid March, he had managed to get contracts signed for the full 500 acres. The flax factory sent out three drilling machines for sowing the seed; after a test at Island Farm, the drills were sent out to other farms, and the co-operators set to and sowed 98 acres by hand!

Later in the year came time to pull the flax.

The four teams were assembled, and from the end of July and throughout August they went forth on each fine day. The four tractors towing the monstrous-looking pulling machines became known as the Panzer Division. We divided it into two sections of two machines each, one section to each field of flax. As far as possible we kept the Panzer Division on the same farm, or if it had only one field of flax, on nearby farms; this was necessary as we had to run our lorry daily from our base at Island Farm to the working point, bringing the crew and its food, and fuel, oil and grease and spare parts for the machinery.

The mechanical pulling of the North Pembrokeshire flax crop went 'according to plan'. When it was all done we were complimented for our neat work and for finishing ahead of all other areas, in spite of having sown our crops generally later than in the south of the county.

But the hand-pulling caused a much greater headache. Soldiers from training camps were promised one day and withdrawn by the time the buses arrived for them. Military law prevented wages being paid direct to the men, who, receiving nothing and being told it was all part of a military exercise, could hardly be blamed for not exerting themselves. Nor did they, save when the farmer gave them something out of his own pocket.

Schoolchildren, being paid anything from 6d. to 9d. per hour, proved to be better than soldiers. In fact, under the supervision of masters and mistresses, their output per head sometimes surpassed that of the soldier. The best team was a holiday camp from Christ's Hospital, Bristol, under the inspiring leadership of Mr Richardson. Irish labour beat all – but they were paid well on piece work, and were saving money to take home to wives and families; unfortunately they were too scarce to have much influence on the total acreage.

In and out of the narrow country lanes, by steep hill, by mountain pass and hanging wood, the grey-painted, thirty-seater buses of the Western Welsh Company found their way to the flax-fields of the North Pembrokeshire farms, bringing to their old-world life a breath of the world of tomorrow. These happy, eager schoolchildren were forever singing the old traditional songs of Wales on their journeys. When the buses reached the farms, boys and girls tumbled out of them excitedly, rushed to fill their water-flasks at the nearest spring, then fanned out along the edge of the golden flax.

"How do we pull it, please, mister?"

The slow ones needed encouragement, the quick ones needed restraining, needed to be taught to help the slow workers and prevented from plunging ahead of others. The good overseer kept the children working smoothly on a broad level front, gave them occasional five-minute rest spells, and saw to it that the kettles and the milk from the farm were brought to the field sharp at noon. At 4.30 the kettles came round again, and at 5 the buses tooted, the children scrambled aboard, and the party returned to their home towns along the seaboard of North Pembrokeshire.

What tales they had to tell of what they'd seen and done! The wild flowers they had collected in the dinner hour, the friendly sheep-dogs, the bull in the shed, how lazy Mairwen had been, how May had cut her finger on the sharp flax-stems, how Eirlys had trod on a toad, how Ifor had fallen asleep under a tree when he had got out of the bus feeling a bit sick, how Caradog had pulled more flax than anyone, and how nice the master had been; and how everyone must be ready again in the square for the bus at 9 a.m. sharp tomorrow.

Yes, although it had been a strain, this organisation of the buses, the soldiers, the children, the voluntary workers and the Panzer Division, yet, looking back on it, it was labour and anxiety well spent. After it was all over, the countryside seemed suddenly empty and less friendly. Everyone had really enjoyed it, even the soldiers who grumbled because they saw none of the money, which, for some reason, had to be paid into the coffers of the W.A.E.C. The life of the countryside had received a healthy stirring, town children had reached remote farms and beautiful country which they might never normally see, and farmers had a glimpse of merry young boys and girls that had made them remember their childhood and what they owed to the future generations.

If only such expeditions could be arranged every harvest-time, if only a sensible Government planned a semi-compulsory labour duty at harvest for all young men and women. What a chance to broaden their lives, enrich their health, and develop the community sense of the people of tomorrow!

Over the next few months, the farmers suffered one disappointment after another: errant sheep ate a crop, a healthy Shire colt strangled itself in a freak accident, a brooder house burnt down, a promised Dutch barn did not turn up, thus making storage of corn very difficult. And then some heifers slid down a cliff, and in trying to rescue them Cyrus slipped, hit his back, and fell into the sea. He was bed-ridden with damaged vertebrae for a year. It was a huge blow. Other difficulties followed. Even the living arrangements, which had to change when Cyrus was unable to participate, were unsatisfactory.

A minor anxiety was the treatment of our linen, silver and furniture at Inland Farm; inevitably it had suffered from the rough clothes and dirty footwear of the male co-farmers who had used it all the summer. Perhaps we had been foolish in giving them free use of the best of our possessions. But to do less was surely not co-operation in its truest form – the sacrifice of personal possessions and personal ambitions for the common good? Eventually, if co-operation succeeded, these things would be straightened out by the goodwill of our comrades, and justice would be done to all of us.

The standard of effort which we talked of was always far above our performance. At first I said very little, knowing how difficult pioneering conditions were at Island Farm, and how easy it was for the man not actually taking much part in the physical work to criticize. There were moments when I felt it would be better to fall back on the local farm labourer, born to a habit of steady work, obedient to a discipline that was self-respecting but not servile. It became clearer to me that perhaps we had gathered together too many leaders and too few servants of the cause.

Uneasy as I was about the immediate future of this band of zealots, and worried about our lack of capital, I yet held to my faith in the ultimate success of a body of enthusiasts who could devote so much love and energy – even where this was at times misguided – to the land. Moreover, I wanted to see this sense of responsibility flowing along the right channels – I had hoped it would quickly reach the point when I should be able to resign the chairmanship and become merely an adviser. After all, I was now nearly forty years old, with other wide interests, with duties as flax fieldsman to the Ministry of Supply, with occasional work for the Admiralty, and with my name on many local advisory and conservational committees. Therefore, thrice in the summer, when things seemed to be going well, with a promising harvest ahead of us, I had tendered my resignation to the executive committee. But my resignation had been rejected each time on the grounds that conditions were not yet right for my leaving the helm.

The co-operative was in despair about the fate of Island Farm. The W.A.E.C. had done nothing to modernise the house, and it was still full of rats. The land was not as productive as that of Inland Farm, where most of the farmers then lived. The flax production work Ronald had taken on was time-consuming (the co-operative had won the contract to drive to the factory all the flax grown in North Pembrokeshire, and had two lorries and two drivers on the task). Ronald had the idea one evening – after once again having his resignation refused – that he and his wife and three of the farmers would take on Island Farm – the house and the farm – leaving the others to run Inland Farm. Everyone loved this idea, and work began.

It was about this time that Lord Woolton [*wartime Minister of Food*] had made his famous statement that farmers must be prepared, if necessary, to lose money on crops this year [*1943*], the year of greatest effort for us all, the year when the road to victory was to open out before us. We must fill up every acre with corn, potatoes and flax, no matter what it cost in sweat, toil and tears, no matter if it were a paying proposition or not.

The Island Farm sub-committee agreed to do their damnedest, and plough out the last marginal acres, including seventeen acres along the eastern cliffs of the island. So 'marginal' were these in fact that we had to plan a decent area as a safety zone on the cliff edge for the turning of the tractor on the headlands.

Pauline was chief ploughman, and could be left safely all day in the most difficult fields. The amount she had ploughed each day could almost be measured by watching her shut the tractor shed door at night. She had been trained to a high standard of performance, and if this was not achieved each day there was a frowning and slamming of doors.

To help with the potato harvest, the W.A.E.C. installed a dozen Women's Land Army volunteers.

Nothing but praise must be accorded the work of the average W.L.A. volunteer. Without them we should have accomplished very much less than we did. But the best types were certainly those which volunteered to go forth and live on the farm and take part in the family life and the farmer's intimate struggle with the land. These girls were often country-bred, appreciate of the open-air life, warm, sincere and noble young women.

The poorer types were the young women, principally born and brought up in towns, who paraded late for work every morning, whose faces were heavily smeared with cosmetics, who walked with lagging steps to the field, who dawdled through their work, who sat down frequently and lengthily, who purposely left their raincoats in the hostel, so that when a shower came they had to run home 'wet through' – while our own land girls carried on – and stayed home for the rest of that day, who asked the time constantly, who sneaked off ten, twenty, thirty minutes before finishing time. Cajoling, teasing, praise or threats had no effect on this hard core of the young female unemployable product of the industrial city, whose brothers and sweethearts were giving their lives on the battlefields of North Africa, the Far East, and at sea. They had no sense of citizenship, no consciousness of the national dilemma, no desire but to shirk work and at all times continue the plotting and planning to secure 'their man' somehow, the principal source of supply being the nearest military camps.

Although the farmers were now polarised, work-wise, they carried on meeting socially once a fortnight, alternately at Inland Farm and Neat House. Machinery and labour were exchanged as required. Then Tommy and Celia got married, and found themselves a small-holding not far from Island Farm. Timothy announced that he wished to concentrate on market gardening, and left for Kent. The Stormson family, Lorry and Lydia, their mother Teresa, and the ailing Cyrus, still farmed Inland Farm, and late in 1943 when the lease ran out they took it over. Ronald became sole tenant of Island Farm. The communal farms experiment had ended.

13

A new future

Spring, the sweet healing season of hope, had come to Island Farm. A year of trial and error was behind us, and now we were tackling the work of sowing the crops and rebuilding the farm.

And, at last, one day the contractors arrived to put up the Dutch barn. In a few weeks they had erected a useful structure 24 ft. wide by 60 ft. long and 20 ft. high, using steel girders and asbestos-cement roofing. It was too late to be of any use this winter, of course. But it would take the 1943 crops, or some of them.

Every morning all of us walked up to the farm from the Neat House through the lovely sheltered lane and wood of Cwm Ynys – the Island Valley. Every morning more primroses appeared, including the large, rich, pink-coloured variety which I had only seen growing in Pembrokeshire. Snowdrops grew in scattered beauty under the leafless trees. Soon yellow daffodils were nodding beside the slender stems of the red campion which, in this mild sheltered place, had not ceased to bloom throughout winter.

Bullfinches were always moving through the tangle of briar and honeysuckle vines, which were already expanding their glaucous green buds. Tree-creepers, long-tailed tits and goldcrests made a thin-voiced, fragile company never absent from the valley, but soon to divide and pair off for the approaching nesting season. Song-thrush and chaffinch shouted their vigorous spring challenges, to be answered by the saw-like song of the great titmouse. Robin, wren and dunnock were part of the orchestra too, but for me the blackbirds' round notes filled out the dawn chorus with the truest harmony.

From high above the wood drifted down the fainter bell-notes of the woodlark, who for hours each find morning drew his horizontal flight-circles in the sunlight, and filled with song the mouth of the warm south-westerly breeze.

In the bank close beside the slippery, clay-bottomed track to the farm several robins had nests. The robin nearest the farm was the tamest. Her eggs were laid early in March. The sitting bird became so familiar that you could life her breast to look at the eggs. These all hatched and the youngsters were fledged by the end of the month.

In mid-March the first summer migrants appeared. The chiff-chaff called from the sallow trees whose catkins were shaken loose by the soft spring weather. And wheatears appeared along the rocky crests of the island.

Goldfinches began nesting in the lichened branches of the bullace trees. Yellow-hammers and linnets retreated to the gorse bushes on cliff and hedge, to stammer and stutter their songs, and flirt for a mate and secure territory for the nest.

Along the cliffs, sustained by the upward air currents, the strong-winged buzzards, falcons and choughs were tumbling in their aerial spring games. But the ravens were already feeding young in two deep stick nests lined with wool; one nest on the west and the other on the east side of the island. The choughs were soon to retreat to their inaccessible cave under the highest headland.

At sea, fleets of razorbills lay patterned on the highly furrowed, dark blue surface close beneath the broken and creviced cliffs in which, during May, the hens would each lay a large, long, pear-shaped, speckled egg.

Such was the 'island' spring, coming to us on the south wind, blowing with a rich salt tang over the deep yellow of the gorse, over the newly ploughed fields, and sweeping with flowers and birdsong through out woods. A spring of great promise and some achievement, to be followed all too swiftly by a summer which, for us, had both triumph and disaster inextricably mixed.

In order to carry out the contract work on the house and buildings, we decided to obtain two Italian prisoners of war for the duration of these jobs. We would put them in the farmhouse, and let them cook for and look after themselves, apart from being provided with one main hot meal each day. Allowing for the usual official delays in such cases, I sent for them a few weeks before we needed them. On the next Sunday, as we were sitting down to dinner in the Neat House, they were dumped on our doorstep. We were asked to sign a receipt for 'the bodies of Francesco and Valentino Vizza', and they were ours.

As it turned out, this alarming introduction was the prologue to one of the happiest working partnerships in Anglo-Italian agreement form that can ever have been known. Both men were sons of Calabrian farmers, used to work on the land, and anxious to prove it. They were industrious, clean and courteous. They were to become part of the family. They lived, worked and had their meals with us. It was a matter of regret that the older Italian, worried about his wife and family during the battle of Italy, eventually had to return to camp.

Valentino stayed on. He was a fine-looking, strong man of twenty-two years. His mother had named him Rudolf Valentino, after the famous Argentino, so much admired by the opposite sex.

My wife agreed with me that the only course for us was to

occupy the Island farmhouse this spring. So in March we bundled the cats out, swept and scrubbed the whole house, and moved in – the Baron, Valentino, Francesco, my daughter and wife and I.

The W.A.E.C. eventually helped out with water for the house. A reservoir was built above the house, and gravity feed would take water down to the house and farm buildings. But that was in the future; in the meantime, Ronald consulted hydraulic engineers about a mechanical ram which would pump the water to the house. It worked, and they revelled in their new water supply.

When we had been forced to evacuate Skokholm Island two and a half years before, we had removed with us some of the relics of the wrecked schooner *Alice Williams*. Now her brass-bound wheel found its old home by the fire in company with the long table (which had been made on Skokholm by the Baron). We fixed the wheel in the wall, intending to gear it to the kettle chain. Above the fireplace we hung the show harness and horse-brasses, finery used only on rare occasions today – a ploughing match or a sale – since agricultural shows were suspended for the duration.

A new future looked ahead. The renovated house at Island Farm was beginning to look pleasant. The long table, set around with the long benches, the settle and the oak chest against the farther wall, windows and pictures lightening the bright walls, flowers on top of the gramophone cabinet, the wheel and the horse-brasses shining, a log fire on the hearth, people bustling in and out; all these things brought the core of the farmhouse – its kitchen – back to vivid life again, and restored vitality and harmony to the house that had lain so long asleep in the long pre-war hibernation of despair.

After the war Ronald had time to consider the farming experiment in terms of success and failure.

Although we sigh for efficient controls, yet we fear bureaucracy and regimentation, and those things that hinder the free expression of our ego. Indeed, the whole experiment described in this book [*The Island Farmers*] shows the swing of the pendulum between the two; on one side our anxiety to come together and control our work by efficient co-operation, on the other our love of personal freedom to think and decide and act for ourselves. This fear of regimentation was possibly one of the more serious of the several obstacles against which our experiment in co-farming had stumbled. True, we had started in war-time, and with the handicap of poor land, remote situation and bad harvest weather. My first mistake had been to suppose that men will carry out the orders of their committees without a strong and efficient leader to interpret and, if necessary, to enforce those orders. Clearly I had not been the right man for the job, and now I wondered whether such a man existed– it is hard for any man to be 100 per cent careful and good about the property of a corporation, of a committee, or of what is not his own.

Now I and my fellow workers in this experiment were back full cycle to private enterprise, all of us convinced that the only permanently successful land husbandry unit is the family group, headed by a man steeped in the traditional lore and ritual of the land, respecting the custom of neighbour help and local pageantry. This unit, often despised and believed to be backward by the large mechanised farmer and the general public, is yet, because of its tenacious love of the land, and its dependence on a large family to provide competent and flexible labour, still the most economic and most likely to survive.

Yet the opportunity is now here for the small farmer to make full use of the war-time created agricultural mutual help societies, and to develop them to meet peace-time conditions, by planned production and standardization of farm goods. By these methods the small farmers of Denmark kept their country prosperous even during the years of enemy occupation.

Our experiment attracted many enquiries of which a great number were from members of the armed forces. What, they asked, could they do to get on the land with little or no capital and experience? Could we advise from the experience of our co-farming venture? The answers lie in the reading of this book. Our original collective farm – the 'Island Farmers' – was for its first year to act almost as a training school for the co-operators who were afterwards to launch out on their own, taking with them the experience and the sense of responsibility acquired with us. If the keen would-be farmer can do the same on the farm training centres which are now being set up by the Government, then there is a good change for these beginners.

Successful farming demands unremitting thought and labour. The farmer and his wife and children must make up their minds that their leisure and their work are the same thing, and find joy in that thought. Every hour not spent on the farm is a step backwards, and an opportunity lost. They must look for their reward in the success of the crops, the condition of the animals, and the sincere praise of their neighbours for both. All this gives the reward of an abiding job and a sense of good citizenship that few other vocations can give in the same deep measure.

Afterword

The extracts selected for this book were chosen for the beauty of their writing and, primarily, for the story of R. M. Lockley from birth until just after the Second World War. Any messages we might pick up about looking after the environment are incidental.

Ronald Lockley yearned for island life as a teenager, lived it as a young man, with a young wife and little girl, and left it only when compelled to; he then adapted to farming on the mainland, and living in close company with a number of other people. These are significant changes, but he was also able to take on organisation of co-operative farming enterprises, enter into negotiations with big companies, and learn new farming methods. An 'islander', then, who was not isolated.

In 1944 Ronald and his wife Doris separated. In 1946 he got married to Jill, from the Channel Islands; after about sixteen years he married again, this time a woman from New Zealand, and emigrated there in 1970. He died in 2000, at the age of ninety-six. His daughter Ann still lives in New Zealand.

Compiling this book has been an enormous pleasure, and I hope R. M. Lockley's readers old and new will enjoy his writing as much as I do. The books used were:

The Way to an Island, publ. J. M. Dent & Sons Ltd, 1941 (reprinted in 1941, 1943 and 1947)

I Know an Island, publ. George G. Harrap & Co. Ltd, 1938 (reprinted in 1938 and 1940)

Dream Island Days, a composite of *Dream Island* (1930) and *Island Days* (1934), publ. H. F. & G. Witherby Ltd (1943)

Inland Farm, publ. Witherby (1943)

The Island Farmers, publ. Witherby (1946)

Letters from Skokholm, publ. Dent (1947)